Creation of the Modern Middle East

Yemen

Creation of the Modern Middle East

Yemen

Sandra Weber

Introduction by
Akbar Ahmed
School of International Service
American University

CHELSEA HOUSE
P U B L I S H E R S
A Haights Cross Communications Company
Philadelphia

Frontispiece: A Yemeni man plays with his falcon while chewing *qat*. The leaves from this small, evergreen bush are chewed by upwards of 80% of the male Yemeni population.

CHELSEA HOUSE PUBLISHERS

EDITOR IN CHIEF Sally Cheney
DIRECTOR OF PRODUCTION Kim Shinners
CREATIVE MANAGER Takeshi Takahashi
MANUFACTURING MANAGER Diann Grasse

Staff for YEMEN

EDITOR Lee Marcott
PRODUCTION ASSISTANT Jaimie Winkler
PICTURE RESEARCHER Pat Holl
SERIES AND COVER DESIGNER Keith Trego
LAYOUT 21st Century Publishing and Communications, Inc.

A Haights Cross Communications ✦ Company

http://www.chelseahouse.com

First Printing

1 3 5 7 9 8 6 4 2

Library of Congress Cataloging-in-Publication Data applied for.

Weber, Sandra, 1961–
    Yemen / Sandra Weber.
        v. cm.—(Creation of the modern Middle East) Summary: A history
of the nation of Yemen and a discussion of its role in the Middle East.
Includes bibliographical references and index. Contents: Unity day—
Arabia felix—A divided territory—North Yemen—South Yemen—
Years of conflict—The Republic of Yemen.
    ISBN 0-7910-6513-8
    1. Yemen—Juvenile literature. [1. Yemen.] I. Title. II. Series.
DS247.Y48 W35 2002
953.3—dc21
                                                                2002008250

Table of Contents

Index to the Photographs

Creation of the Modern Middle East

Iran

Iraq

Israel

Jordan

The Kurds

Kuwait

Oman

Palestinian Authority

Saudi Arabia

Syria

Turkey

Yemen

Introduction

Akbar Ahmed

The Middle East, it seems, is always in the news. Unfortunately, most of the news is of a troubling kind. Stories of suicide bombers, hijackers, street demonstrations, and ongoing violent conflict dominate these reports. The conflict draws in people living in lands far from the Middle East; some support one group, some support another, often on the basis of kinship or affinity and not on the merits of the case.

The Middle East is often identified with the Arabs. The region is seen as peopled by Arabs speaking Arabic and belonging to the Islamic faith. The stereotype of the Arab oil sheikh is a part of contemporary culture. But both of these images—that the Middle East is in perpetual anarchy and that it has an exclusive Arab identity—are oversimplifications of the region's complex contemporary reality.

In reality, the Middle East is an area that straddles Africa and Asia and has a combined population of over 200 million people inhabiting over twenty countries. It is a region that draws the entire world into its politics and, above all, it is the land that is the birth place of the three great Abrahamic faiths—Judaism, Christianity, and Islam. The city of Jerusalem is the point at which these three faiths come together and also where they tragically confront one another.

It is for these reasons that knowledge of the Middle East will remain of importance and that news from it will remain ongoing and interesting.

Let us consider the stereotype of the Middle East as a land of constant anarchy. It is easy to forget that some of the greatest lawgivers and people of peace were born, lived, and died here. In the Abrahamic tradition these names are a glorious roll call of human history—Abraham, Moses, Jesus, and Muhammad. In the tradition of the Middle East, where these names are especially revered, people often add the blessing "Peace be upon him" when speaking their names.

The land is clearly one that is shared by the great faiths. While it has a dominant Muslim character because of the large Muslim population, its Jewish and Christian presence must not be underestimated. Indeed, it is the dynamics of the relationships between the three faiths that allow us to enter the Middle East today and appreciate the points where these faiths come together or are in conflict.

To understand the predicament in which the people of the Middle East find themselves today, it is well to keep the facts of history before us. History is never far from the minds of the people in this region. Memories of the first great Arab dynasty, the Umayyads (661-750), based in Damascus, and the even greater one of the Abbasids (750-1258), based in Baghdad, are still kept alive in books and folklore. For the Arabs, their history, their culture, their tradition, their language, and above all their religion, provide them with a rich source of pride; but the glory of the past contrasts with the reality and powerlessness of contemporary life.

Many Arabs have blamed past rulers for their current situation beginning with the Ottomans who ruled them until World War I and then the European powers that divided their lands. When they achieved independence after World War II they discovered that the artificial boundaries created by the European powers cut across tribes and clans. Today, too, they complain that a form of Western imperialism still dominates their politics and rulers.

Again, while it is true that Arab history and Arab temperament have colored the Middle East strongly, there are other distinct peoples who have made a significant contribution to the culture of the region. Turkey is one such non-Arab nation with its own language, culture, and contribution to the region through the influence of the Ottoman Empire. Memories of that period for the Arabs are mixed, but what cannot be denied are the spectacular administrative and architectural achievements of the Ottomans. It is the longest dynasty in world history, beginning in 1300 and ending after World War I in 1922, when Kemal Ataturk wished to reject the past on the way to creating a modern Turkey.

Similarly, Iran is another non-Arab country with its own rich language and culture. Based in the minority sect of Islam, the Shia, Iran has often been in opposition to its Sunni neighbors, both Arab and Turk. Perhaps this confrontation helped to forge a unique Iranian, or Persian, cultural identity that, in turn, created the brilliant art, architecture, and poetry under the Safawids (1501-1722). The Safawid period also saw the establishment of the principle of interference or participation—depending on one's perspective—in matters of the state by the religious clerics. So while the Ayatollah Khomeini was very much a late 20th century figure, he was nonetheless reflecting the patterns of Iranian history.

Israel, too, represents an ancient, non-Arabic, cultural and religious tradition. Indeed, its very name is linked to the tribes that figure prominently in the stories of the Bible and it is through Jewish tradition that memory of the great biblical patriarchs like Abraham and Moses is kept alive. History is not a matter of years, but of millennia, in the Middle East.

Perhaps nothing has evoked as much emotional and political controversy among the Arabs as the creation of the state of Israel in 1948. With it came ideas of democracy and modern culture that seemed alien to many Arabs. Many saw the wars that followed stir further conflict and hatred; they also saw the wars as an inevitable clash between Islam and Judaism.

It is therefore important to make a comment on Islam and Judaism. The roots of prejudice against Jews can be anti-Semitic, anti-Judaic, and anti-Zionist. The prejudice may combine all three and there is often a degree of overlap. But in the case of the Arabs, the matter is more complicated because, by definition, Arabs cannot be anti-Semitic because they themselves are considered Semites. They cannot be anti-Judaic, because Islam recognizes the Jews as "people of the Book."

What this leaves us with is the clash between the political philosophy of Zionism, which is the establishment of a Jewish nation in Palestine, and Arab thought. The antagonism of the Arabs to Israel may result in the blurring of lines. A way must be found by Arabs and Israelis to live side by side in peace. Perhaps recognition of the common Abrahamic tradition is one way forward.

The hostility to Israel partly explains the negative coverage the Arabs get in the Western media. Arab Muslims are often accused of being anarchic and barbaric due to the violence of the Middle East. Yet, their history has produced some of the greatest figures in history.

Consider the example of Sultan Salahuddin Ayyoubi, popularly called Saladin in Western literature. Saladin had vowed to take revenge for the bloody massacres that the Crusaders had indulged in when they took Jerusalem in 1099. According to a European eyewitness account the blood in the streets was so deep that it came up to the knees of the horsemen.

Yet, when Saladin took Jerusalem in 1187, he showed the essential compassion and tolerance that is at the heart of the Abrahamic faiths. He not only released the prisoners after ransom, as was the custom, but paid for those who were too poor to afford any ransom. His nobles and commanders were furious that he had not taken a bloody revenge. Saladin is still remembered in the bazaars and villages as a leader of great learning and compassion. When contemporary leaders are compared to Saladin, they are usually found wanting. One reason may be that the problems of the region are daunting.

The Middle East faces three major problems that will need solutions in the twenty-first century. These problems affect society and politics and need to be tackled by the rulers in those lands and all other people interested in creating a degree of dialogue and participation.

The first of the problems is that of democracy. Although democracy is practiced in some form in a number of the Arab countries, for the majority of ordinary people there is little sense of participation in their government. The frustration of helplessness in the face of an indifferent bureaucracy at the lower levels of administration is easily converted to violence. The indifference of the state to the pressing needs of the "street" means that other non-governmental organizations can step in. Islamic organizations offering health and education programs to people in the shantytowns and villages have therefore emerged and flourished over the last decades.

The lack of democracy also means that the ruler becomes remote and autocratic over time as he consolidates his power. It is not uncommon for many rulers in the Middle East to pass on their rule to their son. Dynastic rule, whether kingly or based in a dictatorship, excludes ordinary people from a sense of participation in their own governance. They need to feel empowered. Muslims need to feel that they are able to participate in the process of government. They must feel that they are able to elect their leaders into office and if these leaders do not deliver on their promises, that they can throw them out. Too many of the rulers are nasty and brutish. Too many Muslim leaders are kings and military dictators. Many of them ensure that their sons or relatives stay on to perpetuate their dynastic rule.

With democracy, Muslim peoples will be able to better bridge the gaps that are widening between the rich and the poor. The sight of palatial mansions with security guards carrying automatic weapons standing outside them and, alongside, hovels teeming with starkly poor children is a common one in Muslim cities. The distribution of wealth must remain a priority of any democratic government.

The second problem in the Middle East that has wide ramifications in society is that of education. Although Islam emphasizes knowledge and learning, the sad reality is that the standards of education are unsatisfactory. In addition, the climate for scholarship and intellectual activity is discouraging. Scholars are too often silenced, jailed, or chased out of the country by the administration. The sycophants and the intelligence services whose only aim is to tell the ruler what he would like to hear, fill the vacuum.

Education needs to be vigorously reformed. The *madrassah,* or religious school, which is the institution that provides primary education for millions of boys in the Middle East, needs to be brought into line with the more prestigious Westernized schools reserved for the elite of the land. By allowing two distinct streams of education to develop, Muslim nations are encouraging the growth of two separate societies: a largely illiterate and frustrated population that is susceptible to leaders with simple answers to the world's problems and a small, Westernized, often corrupt and usually uncaring group of elite. The third problem facing the Middle East is that of representation in the mass media. Although this point is hard to pin down, the images in the media are creating problems of understanding and communication in the communities living in the Middle East. Muslims, for example, will always complain that they are depicted in negative stereotypes in the non-Arab media. The result of the media onslaught that plagues Muslims is the sense of anger on the one hand and the feeling of loss of dignity on the other. Few Muslims will discuss the media rationally. Greater Muslim participation in the media and greater interaction will help to solve the problem. But it is not so simple. The Israelis also complain of the stereotypes in the Arab media that depict them negatively.

Muslims are aware that their religious culture represents a civilization rich in compassion and tolerance. They are aware that given a period of stability in which they can grapple with the problems of democracy, education, and self-image they can take their rightful place in the community of nations. However painful the current reality, they do carry an idea of an ideal human society with them. Whether a Turk, or an Iranian, or an Arab, every Muslim is aware of the message that the prophet of Islam brought to this region in the seventh century. This message still has resonance for these societies. Here are words from the last address of the prophet spoken to his people:

> All of you descend from Adam and Adam was made of earth. There is no superiority for an Arab over a non-Arab nor for a non-Arab over an Arab, neither for a white man over a black man nor a black man over a white man . . . the noblest among you is the one who is most deeply conscious of God.

This is a noble and worthy message for the twenty-first century in the Middle East. Not only Muslims, but Jews, and Christians would agree with it. Perhaps its essential theme of tolerance, compassion, and equality can help to rediscover the wellsprings of tradition that can both inspire and unite.

It is for these reasons that I congratulate Chelsea House Publishers for taking the initiative in helping us to understand the Middle East through this series. The story of the Middle East is, in many profound ways, the story of human civilization.

– **Dr. Akbar S. Ahmed**
  The Ibn Khaldun Chair of Islamic Studies and
  Professor of International Relations,
  School of International Service
  American University

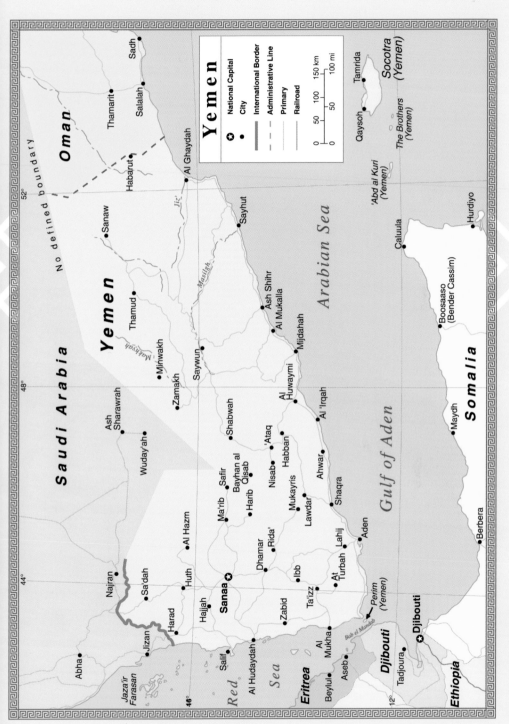

Modern map of Yemen

On Monday, May 22, 2000 in the city of Sana, Yemenis celebrated the 10th anniversary of the unification of northern and southern Yemen.

1
Unity
Day

On May 22, 1990, Ali Abdullah Saleh stood before the large crowd of Yemeni people and listened to them chant, "Unity is power." Above their heads, squadrons of Soviet-built MIG-23 fighters, owned by the old South Yemen, crisscrossed the sky in celebration. Nearly 11,000 people joined hands and rejoiced that the separation of northern and southern Yemen had ended.

At checkpoints along the old north-south border, barrels filled with concrete were rolled away. Crowds cheered that after May 22 there would be no more barrels. This separation had not been their choice; the Ottoman Empire and Great Britain had created the border at the start of the twentieth century.

Unity had been a dream for Saleh and the Yemeni people for a long time. But that dream was always riddled with violence, sabotage, foreign pressures, and other perils. As President of the new Republic of Yemen, Saleh survived dozens of rumored assassination attempts. Now, he stood at the port of Aden, at the southern tip of the Arabian Peninsula, watching his dream of unity become a reality.

The eyes of the world looked on with surprise and bewilderment. The two regimes had such vastly different demeanors and forms of government. The south, known as the People's Democratic Republic of Yemen (PDRY), was Marxist and had a small and poor population. The north, or Yemen Arab Republic (YAR), was a conservative Arab society with strong tribal influences. It had four times as many people as the south, and under Saleh's leadership, its economy was growing. It seemed a wonder these two regimes could unify, and some neighboring nations found it even more shocking that Yemen had adopted a multiparty democracy with an elected parliament and a free press.

The location of this historic unification event, the port of Aden, had a long history of days of excitement, usually in anticipation of revolution and war. Though "Aden" is Arabic for "Eden," this Yemeni city is no paradise. Kingdoms and empires have risen and fallen. A sequence of local sheiks, sultans, and foreign emperors seized power and ruled the city. The Ottoman Turks took the port in the sixteenth century and the British controlled it in the nineteenth century. The Yemeni people fought off the British and gained independence twenty years ago. But, they were aided and influenced by the Soviet Union. In pro-Soviet hands, the port lost Western business and its economy suffered. Then the city was torn apart by civil war.

Aden had been the capital of South Yemen. As of May 22, 1990, it became the economic capital of the unified Yemen. It seemed likely to play a key role in the fortunes of the new country. It has one of the deepest harbors in the world and holds a strategic location, at the southern tip of the Arabian Peninsula at the mouth of the Red Sea. Perhaps a bit ironic is that the city of Aden is scattered around the almost 600-meter-high volcano that forms Cape Aden. The oldest part of the city is called the Crater (or Critit), because it is built in the crater of the extinct volcano. It is surrounded by huge lava mountains that shield the port from winds and bad weather. This makes Aden the best natural port on the Arabian Peninsula. It is a major petroleum storage facility between the Mediterranean Sea and the Indian Ocean.

The other major city in Yemen, Sana, was the old capital of North Yemen and is now the capital of unified Yemen. Sana is located in the central highlands at about 7,500 feet above sea level. On May 22, thousands of people in Sana echoed the joy of unification of their southern partners. They clapped and cheered. They crowded into the national sports stadium for traditional music, dagger dancing, and speeches.

Fireworks filled the sky over Sana. Strings of colored lights hung from buildings. Banners draped from street corners and declared: "Yemeni unity is an immortal victory for democracy, development, and freedom." And a major victory for President Saleh, too.

THE DREAM OF UNITY

If anyone could succeed in unifying Yemen, it was Saleh; his past actions had proven him to be wise and courageous. As a boy, he attended the local religious school and, at age 16, he joined the Armed Forces. Just four years later, in 1962, he was one of the leaders of a military coup against the Islamic monarch of North Yemen. In 1974, he helped to bring Colonel Ibrahim al-Hamdi to power. Three years later Hamdi and his successor were assassinated, and the country was in turmoil. All of the leaders were afraid to take power and serve as the next target of assassination. Saleh finally agreed to take the role. It was an opportunity to save his country but it might also have been the end of his career, even his life. Some said the 36-year-old Saleh would last six months at best.

On July 17, 1978, Saleh was officially elected President of the Yemen Arab Republic (North Yemen) and Commander-in-Chief of the Armed Forces. As expected, a military coup was attempted against him. But he succeeded in fighting it and retained power. In 1983, he was unanimously reelected.

Saleh always promoted the unity of Yemen. Attempts at unification had been made in November 1972, and Saleh attempted it again in March 1979. Agreements were signed, but nothing came of them. Mutual distrust had reigned for many years and was not easily overcome. One conflict after another prevented the unification process from going forward. Border wars broke out in 1972 and 1979. But in the late 1980s, the atmosphere of unification talks seemed different. The recent discovery of oil in both Yemens and the breakup of the Soviet bloc were two major factors.

South Yemen found itself in a position of needing the cooperation of the north. A civil war in 1986 had devastated the PDRY, making it one of the poorest countries in the region. Then the end of the cold war and the collapse of the Soviet Union left South Yemen in a financial disaster. Its principal sources of financial, technical, and personnel assistance were cut off. Meanwhile, its citizens watched as North Yemen rebuilt its republic and, under Saleh's leadership, made its economy stronger and more stable. South Yemen was floundering and its leaders no longer considered unity to be an act of treason. They seemed ready to consider unification with Saleh and North Yemen.

The discovery of oil in both countries and along the undefined border between the two Yemens offered potential wealth. But it also meant more disputes about the border

On July 17, 1978 Ali Abdullah Saleh was elected president of the Yemen Arab Republic (North Yemen). Saleh dreamed that unity would bring peace and prosperity to both north and south.

and the oil deposits. In March 1988, reports circulated that oil exploration teams were surveying in the area for the PDRY and the YAR. Both sides sent armed forces to the area to protect their interests. In mid-April, a summit meeting was held between President Saleh and Ali Salim al-Baydh, the secretary general of the Yemen Socialist Party. On May 4, the two leaders signed major agreements.

These agreements settled the border dispute and established a joint oil exploration area along the border. They also began to link the two Yemens. Specific actions were taken to connect the two electric power grids and to demilitarize the border area. They agreed to open the borders between the two countries, allowing all Yemenis to move back and forth freely. To some observers, merely the fact that the two sides were talking meant a great improvement in mutual trust and some confidence that friendly ties were possible.

A few months later, on November 29, 1989, when Saleh headed to a big delegation of citizens from all over North and South Yemen, he was amazed at the sights along the way. As he approached Aden, people lined the road and cheered for unity. When he entered the capital city, he greeted and waved to the public, who showed their overwhelming support for unity.

The political environment for the socialist party in Aden was extremely precarious and tense. The people were pressing for unity. The socialist leaders were caught in a trap and there was no one to turn to for aid; the socialist regimes were gone.

Saleh commenced discussions with the PDRY (South Yemen) on a proposal for unity. The socialists immediately began to find obstacles. They claimed the Gulf countries, particularly Saudi Arabia, would never allow Yemeni unity, and might try arranging the assassination of all those involved in the unification process, including Saleh. They also claimed that several members of the international community indicated that they were against unity.

Saleh declared that unity must be accomplished at all cost, including the cost of his own life. Even if unity was experienced for just a few days, Saleh felt it was worth a try.

Baydh repeated the socialist party's fears for Saleh's life. He worried that if anything happened to Saleh, war could break out between North and South Yemen, or their

Qat chewing is a national pastime for males in most Yemeni homes. It is a mild stimulant and produces a state similar to that induced by drinking alcohol.

neighbors. It was clear the socialists did not want unity, even though they were aware of the growing support for it among the people.

That afternoon, Saleh met privately with Baydh at his home. They had a *qat* chewing discussion. Qat, a small evergreen bush, is grown at high altitudes in Yemen and chewing qat leaves is a national pastime. It is a mild stimulant and produces a state similar to drinking alcohol.

Qat parties take place in the afternoons in Yemeni houses. Every male has to attend a chew at least once a week or he will be regarded as a social outcast. Although most talk is just everyday chatter, decision-making also requires qat.

During the chew session, Baydh told Saleh that he knew of plans by fundamentalists and tribes in the north to assassinate Saleh. Saleh was not alarmed and persisted in his demands for Baydh's approval of unity. Baydh emphasized the difference between the population of the North and the South. He voiced his concern about the socialist leadership being replaced by former leader Ali Nasir Muhammad.

Saleh asked him to forget about the past, and concentrate on uniting Yemen and its people at all costs. He also recommended the merger of the two governments. Saleh conceded to almost all of the demands of the southern leaders. He offered several members of the socialist party key positions in the new government including the posts of Vice President, Prime Minister, Minister of Defense, and Minister of Oil.

Finally, both men agreed to sign the united constitution and to refer it to parliament for approval. Baydh called party members to an emergency meeting on the agreement. Tensions rose among the divided socialists and one member threatened to kill parliament members if the agreement was approved. The situation seemed too tense for a decision to be made, so two men were sent to convince Saleh to allow more time. Saleh refused. He demanded that South Yemen give approval that night, or else he would publicly disclose the situation to the people. The agreement was signed.

THE BEGINNING OF UNITY

Speaking to the people in Taiz the following day, Saleh asked them to forgive and forget the past. He said that unity did not imply a takeover; therefore, there were no winners or losers. In Sana, Saleh was received by a warm reception,

Sana is an ancient city established before the birth of Christ. For over a thousand years Sana was known only through stories and myths because most outsiders were restricted to staying in ports or other coastal areas.

with people carrying him on their shoulders. The people's reaction was more joyful than Saleh had ever expected.

On January 22, 1990, Saleh was invited to the United States by then-President George Bush. During discussions, Bush asked Saleh: "How can you achieve unity with the Marxists in the south who are enlisted as terrorists?"

Saleh replied: "I guarantee that all kinds of terrorism

from the regime in South Yemen will end when we announce unity. But if we remain two separate countries I cannot guarantee the end of terrorism. Unity alone can put an end to terrorism."

The successful outcome of Saleh's visit to the United States was that he gained Bush's support and commitment for unity, putting more pressure for unification on the leadership in Yemen. Later, Saleh and Baydh met and agreed to speed up the unification process. They also began discussing the allocation of posts and strategies for unity.

The leaders of the two Yemens knew that they were heading into politically uncharted territory. They were undoubtedly aware of the uncertainties of their plans and opposition. They surprised everyone by approving a draft agreement on April 22, a full six months ahead of schedule. The parliaments of the two nations approved the merger on May 21. This paved the way for May 22, 1990, Unity Day for the new country named the Republic of Yemen.

At noon, Saleh performed his first official act as president of the republic; he raised the new flag. It had three stripes: red, white, and black. Red was for the spirit of revolution. White stood for a better future. Black was for the dark days and feudal regimes of the past.

The Republic of Yemen unified two very different political systems. North Yemen was an Arab nationalist government and South Yemen was run by the Yemen Socialist Party (YSP). The new system was a multiparty democracy. During the transitional period before party elections, which were to be held in thirty months, the Republic of Yemen was governed by a Presidential Council. To balance power between north and south during the transition period, the five-member council chose Saleh as president and Baydh as vice president.

Unfortunately, unity did not mean harmony. The agreement to a merger by Baydh and South Yemen had little to do with a real desire for unity. Baydh's participation in the new government seemed to be merely a way for Baydh to save himself. His support for unity was not sincere and he did not wait long for an opportunity to show his displeasure with the new political system.

Just two and a half months after unification, Saddam Hussein invaded Kuwait. The new Yemen government refused to join the anti-Iraqi coalition, and they protested the foreign military forces congregated in Saudi Arabia. Saudi Arabia was angered and therefore expelled about 850,000 Yemeni workers who were residing in Saudi Arabia.

This brought difficulties for Yemen. Unemployment was already high and returning workers added to the problem. The loss of foreign jobs also meant the loss of remittance from these jobs. To make matters worse, Yemen's stance on the Iraqi invasion brought criticism and reduced aid from foreign countries. Political turmoil erupted and Saleh's leadership was questioned.

Yemen had unified under the flag of red, white, and black, but the fragile frame of the new republic was being shaken. Saleh had dreamed that unity would bring prosperity and peace, and that the dark days lay in the past. But dark days of civil war lay in the future, too. In 1994, Baydh would announce the secession of the south. Once again, Saleh would have to piece the dream back together.

Aden is also a city with a long history in Yemen. In the 1880s, when this photograph was taken, it was home to a large camel market. Before there were automobiles, camels transported people and goods around the desert regions.

2
Arabia Felix

Until the 1970s, Yemen was effectively closed to foreign visitors. Only its ports were well known; the interior territory harbored secrets. No railroads crossed the countryside and there were very few paved roads. Instead of cars and trucks, people used horses, donkeys, and camels for transportation in the rural areas. Yemen was an inaccessible and hidden land, shrouded with mystery and tales of ancient riches. Now the veil has been pulled back and Yemen's incredible past comes into view.

A visitor to Yemen might at first think that Yemen is like its Arab neighbors. Its people practice the Islam religion and 98 percent are of Arab descent. Yemen's Arabic name "al-Yemen" actually translates as "southward," meaning south of Mecca. But the similarity of religion, language, clothing, and desert terrain hide the sharp contrasts between this state and the rest of the Middle East. The old South Yemen is the only Arab region that was once a Marxist state. Yemen's current government is the only parliamentary democracy on the Arabian Peninsula. It also stands out as a highly populated and relatively poor country; it is not as rich in oil as its neighboring nations. The Yemeni people are different, too. Even far back in history, they have not been nomads or semi-nomads; most Yemenis live in small villages and do not travel about the country. Thus, local and tribal ties are very strong.

The most surprising and significant difference is Yemen's physical geography. If a visitor ventures between the shoreline and the northern desert sands, it is immediately obvious—Yemen is a unique land.

Yemen is green and grassy, and mountainous, too. Between the peaks, wide plateaus possess abundant rainfall and fertile soil. Farmers raise grains such as wheat, barley, and durra (a cereal grain). They also grow beans, lentils, onions, and tomatoes. Some people raise cotton and tobacco. Orchards grow a variety of fruits, including apricots, bananas, grapes, papayas, and pomegranates. The city of al-Mukha (Mocha) is famous for its coffee groves, which produce a fragrant strong coffee called mocha.

In ancient times, the area now occupied by the Republic of Yemen was known as *Arabia Felix*, meaning happy or prosperous Arabia. This name distinguished it from the lands of Saudi Arabia known as *Arabia Deserta*, meaning desert Arabia.

About 1400 B.C.E., an important trade route began forming in the region. Luxury items such as pearls, spices, ivory, textiles, and ostrich plumes, came from east Africa, India, and China. They arrived by sea at the port of Aden and were loaded onto donkeys. These caravans then passed through Yemen on an elaborate system of roads leading to the markets of the ancient world. About eleventh century B.C.E., the caravan travel through Yemen improved with the introduction of camels, which could walk much longer distances than donkeys without as much rest or water.

Yemen also gained notoriety as a source of two of the most highly prized commodities of the ancient world: frankincense and myrrh. These were produced from the resin of trees, which grew only on the coasts of the Gulf of Aden. Myrrh was an important ingredient in perfumes, cosmetics, and curative treatments. Frankincense was burned as an offering to ancient gods. It was thought that incense could carry one's prayers to heaven. Its use in religious ceremonies, particularly in cremation and burial services, made frankincense a valuable and widely consumed material. Thus, the caravan route through Yemen became known as the Incense Road.

THE LAND OF SABA

Control of the caravan trade and the production of frankincense and myrrh made Yemen a prosperous place. It became the home of a series of powerful states and empires whose wealth was largely based upon their control over Yemen's trade route. The three most famous and largest of these empires were the *Minaean*, the *Sabaean*, and the *Himyarite*. Their periods of authority overlap somewhat, extending from roughly 1200 B.C.E. to C.E. 525.

The most important of these was the Sabaean, that is, the people of Saba or Sheba. The Sabaeans created a powerful coalition of tribes, each with its own chief and each responsible for protection of travelers through its domain. Besides gaining wealth from trade and the

Extensive terracing on the hillsides in northern Yemen allowed successive Yemeni empires to prosper through intensive agriculture.

production of frankincense, the Sabaeans prospered from agriculture. The abundance of farming was made possible by the people's great cooperation and great building skills. They terraced the hillsides and supported the steps of soil with stone walls to prevent erosion. These terraced gardens were a remarkable construction feat but the ancient Marib Dam stands out as even more striking. The dam, created in the eighth century B.C.E., stood for over 1,000 years.

It was built in the Wadi Adana between the Northern and Central Balaq Mountains. The dam had to be very strong so that it could withstand the force of torrential rain and flash floods that occurred in the mountains. Its foundation was dug into the bedrock. Then a stone base was constructed at the bottom in narrow straits to allow the opening of two floodgates. The high wall of the dam was made of soil and covered with rock.

The purpose of the dam was not to store water; its purpose was to divert water from flash floods for irrigation. A network of small gutters led into surrounding farms and orchards. The dam was the heart of a monumental irrigation project and one of the engineering marvels of the ancient world.

The ancient inhabitants of southern Arabia also erected high-rise buildings of mud and stone, some of which still dominate Yemenite villages today. Archaeologists have discovered a private home that towered eight stories above the ground.

The Queen of Sheba (or Saba), known by the name Bilqis, was a powerful woman in the kingdom of Saba, around 950 B.C.E. The story of her visit to King Solomon appears in the Old Testament of the Bible and in the Koran, the holy book of Islam. In one version, a talking hoopoe bird brings news to King Solomon of the prosperous kingdom of Saba and of its queen. She controlled the southern end of the Incense Road, while King Solomon controlled the northern end. It was important for them to form a friendly alliance, so the queen traveled by camel to the court of King Solomon. She asked the king many questions and he answered them all. His great wisdom and his wealth surpassed her expectations. She gave him large quantities of spices, gold, precious stones, and other gifts.

It is said that the king had heard rumors about the queen. Though she was beautiful, it was thought that she had hoofs like a goat. So the king devised a scheme to find out the truth. He built a room with a glass floor such that it looked like a pool of water. When the Queen of Sheba entered the room, she instinctively lifted her skirts to avoid getting them wet. The king immediately saw that she indeed possessed pretty feet, not hoofs. The king was so charmed by her that she became known as "Queen of the Arabs." He gave her all that she asked for and then she returned to her land of Saba.

While various legends contradict each other and no hard evidence proves that the Queen of Sheba ever existed, Yemenis do not doubt the legend. Many Yemen girls are still named Bilqis after the queen.

The Romans began expanding their power and influence into the Red Sea in the first century C.E.. They learned how to use the monsoon winds to travel between the Red Sea and southern Asia. The sea route soon replaced the overland caravan route. Also, with the rise of Christianity, the use of ritual fragrances was abandoned and there was little demand for frankincense. It was not long before Yemen's glory began to dwindle. The result-ing economic decline made it difficult for the Yemeni people to maintain their extensive cities and facilities. The collapse of the great Marib Dam in C.E. 525 gave a symbolic end to the supremacy of the Yemeni empires.

About that time, the king of Ethiopia seized Yemen. When the king died, the Himyarite tribe of southwestern Arabia, with the help of the Persians, rebelled against the Ethiopians and removed them from Yemen. Thus, Yemen came under Persian rule in 575.

Badhan, the Persian governor of Yemen, converted to Islam in 628. Islam's message of unity and brotherhood was probably very appealing in this land of conflicting rulers

The visit of the Queen of Sheba to King Solomon of Israel in 950 B.C.E. is a central story in the history of the Yemeni people. Although there is no hard evidence for the story, it is almost universally accepted as true by them.

and religions. The new faith of Islam spread readily and quickly in Yemen. The Prophet Muhammad sent his son-in-law as governor, and two of Yemen's most famous mosques—in Janadiyah (near Taiz) and the Great Mosque in Sana—are thought to be among the earliest examples of Islamic architecture.

The triumph of Islam was an important event in Yemen history, but it did not bring absolute unity. Islam had split into two main branches: Sunni Islam, who believed that the successor to Muhammad should be elected, and Shia Islam, who believe the title should be hereditary. Yemenis were divided between the two main branches, and within the branches, they belonged to unorthodox sects. The Sunni branch was the Shafi sect and the Shia branch was the Zaydi sect. The Zaydi sect accepted Zayd ibn Ali, Muhammad's great-grandson, as the last legitimate successor to the Prophet. The leader of the Zaydi sect was known as the imam, and his power was without limits. Beginning with the ninth century, the Zaydi Islams greatly influenced Yemen's culture and civilization. At times, they held power, but throughout the centuries, a series of local and imperial rulers contested for control of Yemen, too.

THE AGE OF IMPERIALISM

In the early 1500s, Europe became interested in the lucrative trade between the Far East and the Mediterranean. As a result, Yemen and the Red Sea became an arena of conflict between the Egyptians, the Ottomans, and the various European powers. The Portuguese tried to take the port of Aden in 1513, but failed. Then the Mameluke rulers of Egypt attacked Aden; they were unsuccessful, too.

In 1517, the Ottoman Turks arrived in Yemen. By 1548, they had successfully conquered from Aden to Sana. Business with Europe grew, not only from the long-standing trade of Indian condiments and spices, but from the emerging market for *Coffea arabica*. The distinctive properties of coffee as a beverage were probably discovered at the beginning of the fifteenth century. The coffee beans grown in Yemen's highlands, known as mocha, were especially desired. The port of Mocha on the Red Sea became an important point in the world coffee market.

Conflict occupied most of the sixteenth and seventeenth centuries. The Ottoman occupation ended in 1636

This old illustration shows a servant serving coffee to a group of Yemeni merchants who have set up a camp on their way to Mocha, a port on the Red Sea that was important to the world coffee market.

when the Zaydi imams freed the country. For some time, the Zaydi ruled much of Yemen, but in 1728, the Shafi Sultan of Lahij in southeastern Yemen took over the port of Aden and the south.

By the beginning of the eighteenth century, the redirection of trade brought dramatic changes to the region. The route to Europe around Africa became the standard one. In the meantime, the coffee plant had been smuggled out of Yemen and transplanted to many places throughout the world. Once again, Yemen lost its international importance and its status. Cities such as Aden and Mocha, which had grown to populations of ten thousand or more, now shrank to villages of five hundred. Famine and disease spread across much of Yemen.

Various European powers tried to establish a presence

in the Middle East in the nineteenth century. The most important participants as far as Yemen was concerned were the British.

Relations between the Sultan of Lahij and the British had been civil. Then, in 1839, robbers raided an Indian ship flying the British flag and held its passengers for ransom. The British seized the opportunity to take over Aden. Two warships, with 38 guns and 700 troops, captured the port and annexed it to the British Crown. To protect Aden from the Ottomans, Britain extended its control to the tribal states in the region around Aden. All of southern Yemen was gradually taken over by the British, but real control remained with the local sheiks and sultans. Britain signed treaties with the tribal leaders, in which Britain promised aid and protection from the Turks and the Zaydi imams of the north in return for loyalty from the tribes. The region came to be known as the Aden Protectorate.

In 1849, the Ottoman Turks moved back into North Yemen, from which they had been driven two centuries earlier. The Turks extended their control all the way from Taiz to Sada by 1882 and it seemed that they were trying to lay claim to the whole of South Arabia.

The interests and activities of the Ottoman and British powers in Yemen were greatly increased by the opening of the Suez Canal and the reemergence of the Red Sea route as the standard passage between Europe and the Far East. The Ottoman Turks continued expanding to the north, east, and south. Meanwhile, Aden had become an important coaling port and in the interest of protecting Aden's outlying regions, the British expanded north and east. Eventually, the British and the Ottoman interests clashed. The confrontations were settled by a border treaty.

The treaty established the division between the Ottoman

territories in northern Yemen and the British possessions in southern Yemen. By 1904, the southern part of the border reaching to the Red Sea had been clearly marked; the remainder was undefined. Obviously, the lack of a clearly demarcated border led to decades of disputes and battles. But even the marked border meant little to the Yemeni people; to them the border was simply an invention created by two foreign powers.

Aden Bay, in southern Yemen, has been the port of entry for many visitors to Yemen for hundreds, if not thousands, of years.

3

A Divided Territory

The Turkish and British governments agreed to mark the border between their territories in Yemen in late 1901. The two Boundary Commissions met in February 1902, each escorted by at least 200 men. When the British discovered that the Turks had already taken the disputed land, talks ended. Each side began to gather more armed forces.

By March of 1903, the southern forces numbered over 2,000. The Turks withdrew and peace prevailed for a while. In September, survey work for the border finally started. There were small skirmishes at Dhabri, Awabil, and Nakhlain as work progressed along the border. At Mufalis there was a dispute about which side of the border a tower was on. To solve the situation, the tower was blown up and the owner compensated.

By April 1904, the border had been marked from northeast of Dhala to the Red Sea. Though it was not well marked and not marked at all in the northern area, a borderline now existed between the north and south. Yemen had been divided. Many of the local tribes, however, refused to recognize the border since foreigners created it.

Border disputes were not the only problem for the Ottoman Turks during this period. Toward the end of the 1800s, uprisings against the Turks had increased, especially in the northern regions of Yemen. One of the agitators was Muhammad ibn Yahya Hamid al-Din, who had gained wide appeal because of his popular sermons. In 1890, Muhammad became *imam* (the religious and political leader of the Zaydis) and began to form an alliance among the highland people. The feeling prevailed that the Turks were corrupt and exploiting the poor. Perhaps most important, in the imam's opinion, they were not upholding God's laws.

Muhammad's young son, Yahya, spent time in the service of his father and learned his ways. It was decided that Yahya should succeed his father as imam. Thus, Muhammad decided to have his son marry the sister of the Hashid sheik. This would ensure the support of the Hashid tribe. When Muhammad died in 1904, Yahya became imam.

IMAM YAYHA

Imam Yahya ibn Muhammad Hamid ad-Din assembled a strong military force and attacked the Turks at Sana, causing them great losses. It is estimated that 30,000 Turks were killed in North Yemen in 1905. In a reply to mediation attempts, Yahya wrote that the land of Yemen had been in the hands of his ancestors since the third century and that the people had only the desire "to order the right and extirpate what is loath-some and reprehensible."

After another uprising, the Ottoman Turks, who were troubled by wars elsewhere, recognized the rule of Imam Yahya and signed a peace treaty with him in 1911. He was given free rule in the Zaydi areas of the country and shared control of some areas, but had no control in the Shafi areas, such as Taiz and al-Hugariyyah. This had the ill effect of dividing the country into parts and defeating the idea of nationalism, but it did establish the imam as legitimate ruler in parts of Yemen.

At the end of World War I, the Ottoman forces departed and the north became free of foreign rule. Imam Yahya took over as the ruler of North Yemen, but there was no official recognition of his authority. In addition, there was no agreement on exactly which territories composed the country of North Yemen. None of that mattered to Yahya. He knew he was the ruler of Yemen and he knew what territories belonged to the Yemeni people; he did not need international recognition or border agreements. He was laying claim to the entire territory of old *Arabia Felix*.

While Yahya brought a sense of order and good fortune to his country, he was also known for his stinginess and harshness. He is said to have broken tradition in the royal harem by putting the ladies to work making uniforms for his army. He built up his treasury partly by monopolizing a large part of foreign trade.

Yahya spent nothing on outward appearances; his clothing and palaces were modest. Even the famous Dar al-Hajar (Palace on the Rock) in Wadi Dahr is not luxurious. The palace is an unassuming series of brown buildings with contrasting white latticework set atop a huge pillar of stone. Its grandeur comes from its striking architecture and setting.

Imam Yahya ibn Muhammad Hamid al-Din succeeded his father as *imam* in 1904. This summer home called Dar al-Hajar, or Palace of the Rock, was built for Yahya in the l930s.

The dominant characteristic of Yahya's reign was isolation. After centuries of foreign intervention, manipulation, and subjection, Yahya saw this as an opportunity for Yemen to act as a unit and to protect itself from harmful foreign influences. He instituted a closed-door policy and insisted that no one entered or left the kingdom without his approval.

No development or modern machinery came to Yemen. Yahya excluded foreign technology, foreign investment, and above all, foreign ideas. He allowed few cars, few factories, few books, and no newspapers. He banned music and even jailed one of his sons for riding a bicycle. The trumpets were blown every night at three hours past sunset. This was the signal for everyone to go home and turn in. While such strict control may have been reprehensible from a modernist's point of view, Yahya needed to bring order to the country.

Gaining control over even the traditionally supportive tribes was difficult. The Zaraniq tribe rose in rebellion in 1925 and tried to form as independent state. Yahya's oldest son, Ahmad, restrained them, which gave Ahmad military credentials (later necessary to make his succession to imam acceptable.)

Controlling the tribes was the first step in Yahya's bigger plan. The imam claimed the right to rule all of historic Yemen, including the Najran oasis held by Saudi Arabia, the Asir region held by Idrisi sheiks, and Aden and the protectorates held by the British. Yahya set out to extend his rule as far as possible, both north and south. First, he began to raid areas under British protection.

ADEN AND THE ADEN PROTECTORATES

In the south, the British had retained control since 1839. They considered the port of Aden to be strategically and economically important to their empire. It was such a heavily used coaling station that it was nicknamed the "Coalhole of the East."

When the Turks withdrew from the northern lands in 1918, the British had little presence outside of Aden. They decided that nothing should change and that Yahya would be acknowledged as the ruler north of Lahij. But when Yahya attacked areas outside of the Zaydi territories, the British changed their good-natured policy toward him.

After trying to negotiate and finding that Yahya did not consider the British-Ottoman border arrangement to be binding on him, the British took action. They armed the treaty chiefs and in 1922, began using their air power to attack Yahya's forces. Since negotiations still failed, the British continued bombing. They even bombed Taiz. The imams were forced to retreat since they had no way to fight the aircraft. Yahya negotiated with the British— since he was about to war with the Saudis—and signed the Treaty of Sana on February 11, 1934.

The British decided that keeping the imam out of the south was not enough. They began to spread their influence far beyond Aden since these areas were deemed critical to the functioning of the city. This area extended a hundred miles in both directions from Aden and became known as the Western Protectorate. The British also tried to bring together the unexplored and rebellious areas of Hadramaut, which became known as the Eastern Protectorate.

Groups who signed treaties to become part of pro-tectorates promised loyalty to the British. The rulers could not make any treaties with foreign groups or sell any territories to foreign groups, except Britain. In exchange, the rulers and their heirs were given Britain's promise of aid and protection from the Zaydi imams and foreigners.

Although too young to serve his country, this young Yemeni boy in 1934 shows the preoccupation with guns and other military gear that is typical of many modern-day Yemenis.

Although the imams could offer a Muslim regime instead of the foreign British rule, the aggressive policies and actions of Yahya alarmed many of the local rulers. They probably feared that a takeover by the imams would mean their loss of power and status. On the other hand, the British paid them a subsidy and hinted at the possibility of independence in the future. Therefore, most of the rulers chose to cooperate with the British.

The task of bringing the Hadramaut valley into the protectorates was the result of the labors of Harold Ingrams, a British resident adviser. Treaties had been made with some of the tribes of the Hadramaut before, but the British were unsuccessful in their attempts to establish order throughout the region as a whole. In 1933 the British decided to put forth a major effort to control the Hadramaut, in order to prevent disorder from spreading to the Western Protectorate. Ingrams was sent to the Hadramaut to assess the situation. He reported that there were about 2,000 separate governments in the Hadramaut.

Ingrams went from tribe to tribe, encouraging them to accept a three-year truce. He obtained 1,400 signatures in this way, and when heavy rains fell that spring, it was regarded as a good omen, and more tribes signed. Ingrams became the first resident adviser to the Eastern Protectorate. He helped establish some basic public services and a sense of peace. In an area where some people had been afraid to leave their homes, this was a great accomplishment. This period became known as *Ingrams' Peace*.

It was later realized that the British misunderstood the method of rule in this area. The ruling families were not really governors but more like mediators. Furthermore, it was not a single person who held authority, but a group of male elders. The ruler or chief position was not handed down from father to son, instead the best candidate was selected by the ruling family.

The effect of Ingrams' Peace was that by signing an agreement with the British, the current ruler and their heirs were frozen into power. The tribal system of selecting the strongest and most effective rulers was gone. In effect, the

British had undermined an important component of the social structure of the region.

The British made a similar blunder among the Aden community. They failed to recognize that the development of Aden was in strong contrast to the tribal areas around it. The city was rapidly changing and modernizing. Its population included many non-Muslims and even non-Arabs. It had a sophisticated business community, activist trade unions, and other modern political and social organizations. Adeni citizens perceived their neighbors in the rural countryside to be largely illiterate and parochial tribal leaders.

When the British developed a new plan for Yemen in the mid-1950s, they seemed to ignore these differences among the people. By insisting that Aden merge with the hinterland, the British created hostility among the people.

THE SAUDI WAR OF 1934

As soon as the British signed a treaty with Yahya and established the southern frontier, Imam Yahya turned his attention to the north. In negotiations with Saudi Arabia, Yahya refused to accept anything except the whole of Asir, a territory bordering North Yemen. War erupted and North Yemen suffered a fast and decisive defeat. However, Yahya was not forced to make any territorial concessions beyond the Asir province. Per the treaty made in May 1934, he only had to give up claims to Asir and to the Najran oasis. Border markers were placed as far as the Najran Oasis but not beyond. To the east was a "no man's land" between Yemen and Saudi Arabia.

In the war with the Saudis, Yahya had been disappointed in the performance of his forces. He recognized that he needed a modernized regular army. So he sent Yemenis to Iraq for education and training. Unfortunately, when they returned, most became involved in politics and tried to change Yahya's policies. His isolationism and exclusion of modern development disturbed them. It was said that Yahya never left the Zaydi highlands and never saw the sea from the Yemeni coast. This lack of worldly vision shocked the young Yemenis and alienated them from the imam.

It is said that Yahya told a visitor that "I would rather that my people and I eat straw than let foreigners in." But he would trade with foreigners for things that he needed, such as weapons and military supplies. He turned to the United States but did not meet with success. Then he asked the Italians who did sign a treaty in 1926 and supply weapons and other facilities.

Though Yahya's methods seem strange, he largely succeeded in creating an independent Yemen, governed by an imam, and enforcing the doctrines of Islam. He also succeeded in grooming his son for the role of imam. His son, the Crown Prince Ahmad, had his seat in Taiz, the second capital. By the 1920s, Ahmad was already an imposing figure. He was more of a warrior than his father, and was also a wit and a poet. However, he made himself disliked and feared in the region by imposing heavy taxes and imposing severe penalties. Once his father sent him a message: "Oh, Ahmad, the people are weary of your cruelties."

Resentment of Ahmad, and of Imam Yahya, was growing. Young Yemenis, particularly those who had been educated abroad, continued to frown on the imam's resistance to modern ways. Others were angered about his handling of commerce and his monopoly on trade. Those in the southern towns close to the metropolis of Aden saw the flourishing commerce of that city and were discontented

Yahya's son, the Crown Prince Ahmad, succeeded Yahya as imam when the father was assassinated in 1948. In Yemen the position of imam was not necessarily passed from father to son and there was resentment in many quarters that this family considered it a hereditary position.

with Yahya's economic policies. Some resented his efforts to make his son Ahmad the next imam. None doubted Ahmad's ability; he was well known as a warrior and a scholar, but the imam position was not customarily passed by hereditary. There were well-qualified men from other families who aspired to be imam.

Some of the dissidents were sent to jail. When they were released, many moved to Taiz where Crown Prince Ahmad ruled. They stayed until 1944 when Ahmad made a statement implying that the blood of the modernists would be upon his sword. Several of the young Yemenis fled to Aden and formed the Free Yemenis group. Among their demands of Yahya was that he permit a constitutional council of lawyers and remove all his sons from positions of tribal ranks. Imam Yahya refused and set out to destroy these opponents. However, a few months later, Imam Yahya was surprised to learn that one of his sons, Prince Ibrahim, had joined the rebels and become one of their leaders.

THE COUP OF 1948

The Free Yemenis decided to assassinate Imam Yahya. On January 17, 1948, rebels were successful in getting into his palace in Sana, but they were discovered and their plan thwarted. The rebel leaders did not know the plan had failed and told the world that the Imam Yahya was dead. The false news spread around the world. Finally, the truth was revealed, but there would be another chance.

In February, assassins ambushed the 80-year-old Yahya as he toured the countryside in his Cadillac. Though the car had bulletproof glass, the gunmen battered the car with machine gun fire. Yahya died, with fifty bullets in his body. However, part of the plan failed; the assassins did not kill Crown Prince Ahmad. He escaped to Hajjah with 180 soldiers and a truck full of money and gold. Many tribesmen came to his aid, partly because of the money he carried with him to buy loyalty and partly because they were shocked at the brutal murder of Imam Yahya, who had been their spiritual leader and the man who had ousted the Turks.

Meanwhile, the Free Yemenis marched to Sana and Abdullah al-Wazir was proclaimed the leader of North Yemen. He did not last long. Opposition forces stormed Sana under the call of "God preserve the Imam!" On April 8, 1948, Abdullah al-Wazir was executed and his head displayed as a warning to others. Imam Ahmad became ruler while his brother Prince Ibrahim was sent to prison.

In Taiz, people lined the road for Ahmad's victory parade, and shouted blessings and words of support. It was said that strange birds flocked into the city. No one had ever seen these birds before, and no one ever saw them again.

These castle buildings in northern Yemen give an air of antiquity to the modern-day Yemen.

4

North Yemen

mam Ahmad was short and stocky with bulging eyes. He wore a forked beard with one prong longer than the other one. He had proven himself to be a great warrior, and though his eerie appearance may not have shown it, a great scholar and poet, too. But he had a fierce temper that could enact cruelty, even on his own son.

Although Ahmad had indicated that he supported reforms of the archaic political, economic, and social systems, when he came to power, his own government closely resembled that of his father. Ahmad concentrated all administration functions at the capital, which he moved to Taiz. He even retained some of the old, oppressive practices. For example, he kept hostages who were sons of the sheiks of the more important tribes. The imam required that these boys be sent to his court, professedly for education. They were given an excellent education but really they were held as a way to secure the good behavior of their fathers.

He showed some human compassion. Many slaves were freed. Many of the liberals who had been jailed in 1948 were released, especially those who could compose a nice poem or a flattering speech. Ahmad let in some foreigners, allowed young people to study abroad, and brought in foreign machines, such as airplanes. In general, though, he continued his father's policy of isolation.

The ability of the two imams, Yahya and Ahmad, to insulate Yemeni society from the modern world and to maintain an independent Yemen rested to a large degree on the agricultural and social systems within the country. North Yemen produced self-sustaining quantities of food and water. Very little external trade needed to be enacted. There was no influence by mass media. There were no political parties or lobbying groups as in more modern political systems. Officials or family heads handled demands, gave rewards, and settled other situations. Often, the imam himself managed these tasks.

Yahya and Ahmad were also successful in securing the country's borders and strengthening the feelings of nationalism. They kept alive the claim of the imams of the Hamid al-Din family to hold authority over all the land and people of Yemen. This meant all the lands once ruled by their family throughout the centuries.

Ahmad still planned to join Aden and the protectorates with North Yemen since he considered these lands part of historic Yemen. In 1953, when Ahmad learned of a British plan for the federation of these lands, relations with the south completely deteriorated. Yahya feared that if these lands became federated, they would be far more difficult to conquer.

The Arab League and Egypt did not support the new federation plan of the British, either. They supported Ahmad. From 1954 through part of 1955, the north maintained contact with rebel groups in the south and aided them with money and arms.

Besides the trouble with the British, Ahmad had trouble within. In 1955, a military coup attempt was made on Ahmad. It was led by the army chief of staff and supported by the imam's brother Abdullah. Six hundred soldiers surrounded Imam Ahmad at his palace. He had no water or electricity. All communication from the outside was cut off. Ahmad was forced to hand over power to Abdullah.

Meanwhile, Ahmad's son Badr rushed to his father's stronghold of Hajjah and raised forces. As he led the troops toward the palace to free Ahmad, somehow the imam escaped by himself. One story is that he grabbed an automatic rifle from one of the soldiers and got free. Ahmad was restored to power and the conspirators were executed.

This event increased his mistrust of the army and the royal family and heightened his repression of the people. However, it did restore Imam Ahmad's faith in his son Badr. Ahmad began to work to ensure his succession as imam, even though Badr was ill qualified. Badr lacked expertise in Islamic law, held reformist ideas, and lived an untraditional lifestyle.

The uprising also convinced Ahmad that he needed to develop some kind of a relationship with surrounding countries. In April 1956, he made his first trip out of Yemen. He met President Nasser of Egypt and King Saud of Saudi Arabia, and the three men signed an agreement known as the Jiddah Pact. Its main goal was to defeat British plans for the federation of Aden and the protectorates.

As a measure of goodwill, Ahmad sent Badr to Cairo to

Tribesmen joined forces with Imam Ahmad to fight the British in 1957.

meet with President Nasser. Badr was greatly impressed by Nasser and believed that Nasser sympathized with him. They even arranged for military training for Yemeni soldiers.

THE DOWNFALL OF IMAM AHMAD

By 1958, Imam Ahmad was ill and relying heavily on Badr. Partially because of Badr's pro-Egypt sentiments, Yemen symbolically joined Egypt and Syria in an alliance called the United Arab Republic. This kept the modernists in Yemen happy, but alienated the traditional tribesmen who were already upset that Ahmad had let so many foreigners into the country.

Despite Badr's amiable relationship with Nasser, Ahmad remained wary of Egyptian intentions. When leaflets appeared that opposed the regime, Ahmad expelled the Egyptian officers who were training troops in Yemen. Then, Ahmad took ill and went to Rome for treatment. Ahmad had suffered for many years from rheumatism and arthritis. His doctors and wives were eager to reduce his pain and kept him supplied with morphine. He had become addicted to the drug and went to Rome to relieve his pains as well as to kick his addiction.

Badr was put in charge while his father was in Italy. Badr, as well as many in Yemen, never expected the Imam Ahmad to return. They suspected he was near death and had passed the throne to Badr.

With Badr in charge, some elements of society were worried. Badr called back the Egyptian officers expelled by his father. He also established a seven-member representative council, began to reform the civil service and the taxation system, and started other changes. He gave gifts and large sums of money to buy peace among some tribes. Other reformers now spoke out and pushed for progress. But instead of supporting Badr's reforms, they made demands of their own and started rioting.

Then Imam Ahmad fooled everyone and regained his health. He was enraged about the changes made by Badr and the incidents that had occurred. Upon returning to North Yemen, Ahmad undid all of Badr's reforms, which humiliated Badr. Ahmad threatened to cut off the heads of the leaders of the insurrection and required the tribes to return the money. He invited a sheik and his son to come and discuss the matter. They were given a safe-conduct pass. After a disagreement, Ahmad ordered both of them beheaded. This action dishonored the merit of the imam's safe-conduct pass. Several groups never again backed the imam because of his reprehensible behavior on this occasion.

On March 26, 1961, another assassination attempt was made against Ahmad. While the imam was at the Ahmadi Hospital for an X-ray exam, he visited some patients. Three men opened fire on him in the stairway. As bullets struck his body, the imam threw himself to the floor. The assassins fled, believing that Ahmad was dead from the five bullets that had hit him.

Once again, he fooled everyone and survived. One bullet went through his right shoulder and into the left. Two had entered his thigh and lodged in his bladder. His head had been injured when he fell to the floor. Miraculously, he was alive.

Ahmad remained very weak and in October, he publicly called on the people to follow Badr and announced his wishes for Badr to succeed him as imam. Just as Ahmad's appointment by his father alienated the traditional members of society, so did Badr's appointment. Heredity was inconsistent with the Zaydi doctrine, and more importantly, many felt that Badr was unqualified.

Hoping to win back support, Ahmad nullified the arrangements with Egypt. He broke off all ties with Nasser. Ahmad was now Egypt's enemy and the Egyptians began to prepare for a revolt in North Yemen.

There were many dissident movements trying to remove the existing government. They included army officers and civilians. Among the civilians were Shafi merchants, young intellectuals, a few industrial laborers, and expatriate dissidents. The most powerful faction was a group of young army officers who formed the Free Officers Organization. They tried to win the support of the tribal sheiks in the Zaydi highlands. Some sheiks of the Hashid gave alliance to the dissident forces because of the

Abdullah al-Sallal dominated the Yemeni government from 1962 to 1967 after King Ahmad's son Badr was overthrown in a revolt.

"safe-conduct pass" incident when Ahmad beheaded a visiting sheik. The officers' organization also established relations with Egypt and Nasser began to move against Ahmad.

The young officers chose Colonel Abdullah al-Sallal as their leader. Sallal was one of the first Yemenis sent for training in Iraq. Then, he had been in jail for participating in the 1948 coup. It was Badr who had urged that Sallal be released because he was a "well-meaning" reformist. In 1961, Badr made Sallal the commander of his personal guard, believing that Sallal would never betray him.

When Imam Ahmad died in his sleep on September 19, 1962, Badr became the Imam of Yemen. At the young age of 35, he was the absolute ruler of four million Yemenis and the entire countryside——for one week.

Badr believed that he could lead Yemen out of the isolation his father and grandfather had imposed and yet still preserve the virtues of the past. He believed he could bring this profoundly traditional kingdom into the twentieth century. But his reign was unsuccessful because he was thought to be incompetent. Thus, the promises of reform made in his speech from the throne were not taken seriously. The revolutionaries were not listening; they were already working to overthrow Badr.

THE COUP OF 1962

Imam Badr had been warned about the danger of assault but refused to believe the reports. One warning advised him that Sallal was one of the officers planning a revolt. Badr did not listen. He called in Sallal and told him about the warning. Of course, Sallal laughed and denied the plot. He assured the imam of his loyalty to him. Badr believed his trusted friend.

On the night of September 26, 1962, the officers took action. They bombarded the Bashair palace in Sana where Badr was staying. Tanks surrounded the building and then shells crashed through the walls. Badr grabbed a machine gun and began firing at his attackers. His gun was useless against the armored tanks, but it showed that Badr was going to put up a fight. The battle continued until the palace lay in ruins. The assailants thought that Badr was buried in the rubble. The radio announced his death and declared a new republic: The Yemen Arab Republic (YAR).

Once again the assailants spoke too soon; the imam was alive. Badr had escaped through the garden and into the back streets. He fled to the northern highlands and rallied the warrior tribesmen to his cause. It seems that most of the traditional highland tribes still preferred imamic rule, however harsh it may be, to rule under foreign influence.

In November, when it became widely known that Badr was alive, the scope of the conflict became evident. The short and simple revolution was about to become a long and bloody civil war. This domestic spat between the supporters of the imam, known as the royalists, and the republicans attracted foreign attention. The republicans were backed by Egypt, and at times the Soviet Union and the United States. Saudi Arabia and Jordan backed the royalists.

The Egyptians sent troops and supplies to Yemen within the first days of the coup. Nasser thought the royalist forces could be defeated quickly and change would come to Yemen. But like many before him, he misunderstood the pattern of politics in Yemen. A tribe or group of supporters often changed alliance, sometimes simply choosing the highest bidder, sometimes swayed by the tide of the battle, sometimes they held to a long-standing grudge or a slight to their honor. But most Yemenis could be quickly united if faced with foreign rule.

The Saudis never sent troops to Yemen but provided the royalists with money and weapons. They wanted to see Egyptian troops removed from the Arabian Peninsula and a return of the monarchy. By the end of 1962, the royalist forces had made some territorial gains. They held the north and east while the republicans held the south and west.

CIVIL WAR

The years from 1962 to 1967 were marked by Sallal's complete domination of the government and Egypt's domination of Sallal. To some in Yemen, it seemed that the Egyptians were getting out of control. They were trying to make improvements in health care and education but they were also authoritarian and causing heavy damage in royalist areas. Egypt's military defense of the republic had evolved into what amounted to Egyptian occupation of Yemen, leaving little room for Yemeni national politics to develop. Yemeni republicans ended up fighting among themselves, and conspiring with or against the Egyptians.

By 1965 the Egyptians were feeling despair. Casualties were high. They had won little territory beyond Sana, the cost of the war was draining the treasury, and they had almost 60,000 troops assigned to Yemen. The war was stalemated. Egyptian President Gamal Abdel Nasser and King Faisal of Saudi Arabia called a cease-fire in August 1965 and began to negotiate a compromise. More meetings were held in November, but no agreement was reached. Fighting resumed in 1966.

By mid-1966 Sallal was ill, but still strong enough to jail some moderates within his government. More arrests followed. Schools, government offices, and barracks were converted to jails. Egypt began to use napalm and poison gas to bomb dissident tribal areas. These methods were distasteful to the Yemeni people, who detested foreign rule in any form. Sallal's rule was becoming unpopular. It was not so much that people supported the royalists, but they started to distrust the republic.

By 1967 both sides were in bad shape. The economy was faltering and there were food shortages. The third consecutive year of drought added to the problem. Farm fields lay fallow. Goats and sheep had died of thirst. People begged for a scrap of bread or a sip of water.

Then, in June 1967, Israel defeated Egypt and this meant a disaster for Nasser. He could not afford the war in North Yemen. Also, he was forced to go to the Saudis for financial support. They agreed, on the condition that Egypt withdrew from North Yemen. Egyptians troops left in October 1967.

Sallal left for Moscow and then went to Iraq. His position as President of North Yemen was filled by Abdul Rahman al-Iryani. But just because Sallal was gone and Egypt and Saudi Arabia had pulled away, the civil war had not ended.

By early December, the royalists circled Sana and made an attempt to take the city. Republican forces fought them off, but royalist forces continued to hold the highlands. Neither side could obtain complete victory. Finally, in 1970, an agreement was reached. The Compromise of 1970 established a republican government with some positions assigned to royalists. However the imam and his family were not to have any role in the new state. Imam Badr went into exile in Britain.

The port of Aden from the air in 1962, the year that it joined the British-created Federation of South Arabia.

5

South Yemen

By the 1950s, Britain's interests in South Yemen consisted of the Colony of Aden and the Protectorate of Aden, which included the Western Protectorate and the Eastern Protectorate. The British exercised very unequal treatment between Aden and the hinterland. Their main interest was the port of Aden; the hinterland simply served as a buffer zone to Aden.

The British made efforts to modernize the town of Aden. There was small industry, education, commerce, and some social services. A middle class was emerging. So were new political parties and labor unions. A legislative council was established, and beginning in 1955, four members of the council were chosen by the Aden people in a general election.

Meanwhile, the British did not want to waste the time and money to control the outlying areas, so they ruled the hinterland indirectly through Residents and Political Agents. The people were largely ignored and left to the whim of these local rulers. Thus, these lands remained susceptible to conflict with North Yemen. The imams continued to claim their rights to the territories. Imam Ahmad became more aggressive when he learned of the British plan to form a federation of states in South Yemen.

By the late 1950s, an earlier proposal to federate some of the smaller states in the protectorate had grown into a much broader scheme. The new federation concept included all of the principalities and sheikdoms. The plan was to unite them into a larger political entity that would eventually achieve independence. It was also thought that Aden should be merged into the federation.

This new political scheme was necessitated by the changes happening in the 1950s. The British constructed an oil refinery at the port of Aden in 1954 and the town was growing rapidly. By 1957, it was one of the largest petroleum bunkering (storage) facilities in the world. It was also a vital fueling stop for ships on the Asian and African routes from the Mediterranean.

The construction and operation of the port facilities created many jobs. Many of the laborers were peasants from North Yemen and the protectorates. But the nature of the jobs made them vulnerable to changes in external conditions. The workers might suddenly find themselves unemployed. They also felt disenfranchised. The British did not allow the non-Adenis workers from North Yemen to vote in the legislative council elections, but other non-Adenis, such as Britains and Indians who could meet a residency requirement, could vote. This grieved the workers and many joined the unions, such as the Trades Union Congress (TUC).

The British constructed this oil refinery at the port of Aden in 1954. It refined crude oil from the Persian Gulf sheikdom of Kuwait.

In March 1956 there were 30 strikes in Aden. In the late fall of 1956, the Suez Canal was closed, causing unemployment and more unrest. There were stirrings of nationalism and protest of British rule. Yet, Aden's service-oriented economy was almost totally dependent on British financial aid, port and bunkering revenues, trade income, and other income stemming from the British presence in Aden.

For the British, Aden had greatly increased in importance as a port and military base. They wanted to strengthen their position in the area but they also needed to do something about the nationalist sentiment that was rising. It seems that the British decided that uniting Aden and the grouping of some 1,300 tribal chiefs in the hinterland and giving them limited self-government would satisfy both of these situations.

Many Yemeni people thought differently. They wanted to establish their own sovereign state and were not eager to join the federation.

The British tried to convince states about the benefits of the federation and reminded them that if a federation came to be, the states outside it would be at a great disadvantage economically and security-wise. The rulers did not want to listen. Ironically, the person who eventually convinced some of the states to become part of the federation was Imam Ahmad.

In 1957, Imam Ahmad delivered weapons from North Yemen to tribes of the protectorate to use against the British. However, as the imam's ties with Egypt increased, the rulers sided with the British, fearing that the imam was securing Egypt's help against the protectorates. They suspected that his real plan was to bring them under his rule. The rulers calculated that their best chance for sovereign rule lay with the British promise of federation.

FEDERATION OF SOUTH ARABIAN EMIRATES

On February 11, 1959, the British created the Federation of South Arabian Emirates as a self-governing territory under British protection. The six founding states were the Dhala emirate, the Audhali sultanate, the Upper Aulaqi sheikdom, the Beilhan emirate, the Fadhli sultanate, and the Lower Yafai sultanate. In October, Lahij joined the federation. This was important since it was the largest state of the Western Protectorate and had about 25 percent of the population. Early in 1960, the Lower Awaliq sultanate, the Dathinah confederation, and the Aqrabi sheikdom joined. The federation scheme seemed to be succeeding in the hinterland, but now Aden needed to be included.

The existing legislative council in Aden was scheduled to end in January 1963 and Aden would be left without a government. Therefore a decision about Aden's merger with the federation had to be completed in 1962. But merging the city of Aden with the hinterland was not easy. As mentioned earlier, many differences existed between the two entities. But despite all the differences, Aden and the hinterland were dependent on each other. Aden was a city without a country and the hinterland was a country without commerce or central administration. It seemed that the two areas needed to join together.

Getting everyone to agree to the conditions of the union was a long and difficult process. The British put heavy pressure on the legislative council to unite Aden and the federated states of the hinterland. The agreement was finally pushed through. On September 26, by a margin of one vote, the council agreed that Aden would join the federation, which would now be called the Federation of South Arabia. This union would come into force on March 1, 1963.

The timing of this agreement proved to be more critical than anyone had realized. One day's delay would likely have meant disaster. By then, the people would have heard that on the night of September 26 a coup was made against Imam Badr in North Yemen. The Yemen Arab Republic was declared. The north had achieved independence from the royal monarchy.

In the south, the British continued to insist upon their chosen course of action—federation. In 1964, Britain announced that the federation would be given independence in 1969. By 1965, all but four of the twenty-one protectorate states had joined the federation. However, its fate was now uncertain; a revolution had started in South Yemen.

SHABI AND THE NATIONAL LIBERATION FRONT

On October 14, 1963, the National Liberation Front (NLF) announced its plans to use force to oust the British. The day is now celebrated as Revolution Day. Military action began in Radfan, north of Aden. For months, NLF snipers fired against the British troops.

At first, neither the British nor the local rulers saw the NLF as a serious threat. It seemed to be just another security problem. The principal organizers of the NLF were tribesmen of Lahij under the leadership of Qahtan al-Shabi and his cousin, Faisal Abd al-Latif al-Shabi. It was a loosely organized group, without a strong ideology.

The NLF had many factions from both Aden and the protectorates. It included the Yafai Reform Front, the Mahrah Youth Organization, the Nasserite Front, the Adeni Revolutionary Vanguard, the Secret Organization of Free Officers and Soldiers, and other such organizations. It also drew support from the Egyptian government.

The various groups had begun to coalesce under the leadership of Qahtan al-Shabi in 1963. But there was not complete harmony. Splits seem to have always existed within the NLF organization. The first major split grew out of disputes between followers of Qahtan al-Shabi who were committed to Nasserism and the second level of young NLF members who were turning more to Marxism. This second level was a more radical faction, encouraged by a small communist group in Aden, the Popular Democratic Union (PDU).

The splits within the NLF were pushed aside while the organization waged war against the British. The conventional British forces had trouble responding to the guerilla tactics employed by the NLF forces, which did not try to gain control of a region but simply engaged in violent acts to make the British campaign costly and dangerous. It took the British over six months to subdue the guerrilla fighters in Radfan. Meanwhile, violent resistance to the federation spread to other areas.

Political unrest seemed to be spreading, too. In Aden, another national group struggled for power. Abdullah al-Asnaj led the People's Socialist Party, which advocated peaceful change in Aden and the protectorates. In May 1965, his group merged with the conservative South Arabian League and became the Organization for the Liberation of the Occupied South (OLOS). This merger caused many radical Adeni workers to leave Asnaj and his organization.

Nasser wanted to unite the anti-British groups and bring them under his influence. The Egyptians kept pressing the NLF to merge with OLOS. In August 1966, NLF leaders Qahtan al-Shabi and Faisal al-Shabi signed an agreement to join with the OLOS and form the Front for Liberating Occupied South Yemen (FLOSY). However, the more radical NLF members rejected the merger. They were angered at Egyptian pressure and threatened the leadership with a split in the organization and loss of control unless the NLF withdrew from FLOSY. This group of radicals included most of the men who would become the leaders of South Yemen in 1969: Abd al-Fattah Ismail, Muhammad Ali Haytham, Salim Rubay Ali, Ali Antar, and Ali Salim al-Baydh.

In November 1966, the older leaders agreed to end their association with Asnaj and FLOSY. The NLF formed its own 15-man executive under Shabi. Now, the NLF was as

Egyptian president Gamal Abdel Nasser hugs a Yemeni soldier while Sallal looks on (right). The years from 1962 to 1967 were marked by Egypt's domination of Sallal. Many in South Yemen felt that Egypt's defense of the republic had evolved into an occupation of it.

much at war with FLOSY as with the British authorities. The reunited NLF was in a strong position throughout the protectorates and in Aden, but the differences within the organization remained and would erupt again.

After the NLF broke away from FLOSY, Egypt supported FLOSY against the NLF. The Egyptians felt that Shabi was difficult to deal with and feared he would become an impossible ally. But the Egyptians' support of FLOSY backfired because it pushed the people to support the NLF rather than the possibility of being ruled by the Egyptians. It also hurt that FLOSY was seen as predominately an Adeni organization, whereas the NLF had links to the hinterland.

In early 1966, the British announced that they would withdraw all forces by 1968 and that there would be no defense treaty with the federated states. The local rulers would be on their own. This set off a violent power struggle that lasted two years. The nationalist groups fought with full force for the control of South Yemen. In secret meetings, the British and NLF agreed to exterminate the FLOSY element. To the British, the NLF seemed the lesser evil versus the influence of Nasser. By August 1967, the NLF was in control of most areas and on the verge of victory over both the British and its FLOSY rivals.

The British began negotiations with the NLF in Geneva on November 21. On November 29, the last British troops left Aden. At midnight, the start of November 30, 1967, the People's Republic of South Yemen was declared.

INDEPENDENCE FROM BRITISH RULE

The new nation was in dreadful circumstance. Its social structure was completely torn apart. Its economy was ruined and Britain gave very little of the money it had promised for rebuilding. Trade through the port was at a standstill. Income from the British base was gone. The new leadership of the NLF was already divided. The British-trained army was of questionable loyalty to the leadership. Standing at the nation's borders were the defeated members of the nationalist movement and their supporters from neighboring North Yemen and Saudi Arabia.

Qahtan al-Shabi became chairman of the presidential council, prime minister, and commander of the armed forces. His cousin Faisal became secretary general. Diplomatic relations were established with many Arab states and Yemen joined the League of Arab States and the United Nations. Traditional tribal boundaries within the country were abolished and the territory was divided into six governorates.

One of the toughest struggles for Shabi came from within the NLF, now called the National Front (NF). The radical group within the NF did not want gradual change of the existing system; they wanted every part of the old system removed, including the old federation army. Among their other demands was unification with North Yemen on NF terms.

In March 1968, at the Fourth Congress of the NF, the radicals had all their positions adopted as resolutions: collective decision making, the purge of the army and civil service, a centrally planned economy, and confiscation of land owned by waifs, wealthy peasants, or traditional landowners. Shabi retained control of the army, which still supported the president. When conflict broke out in Aden, the army put down the revolt and jailed prominent radical leaders, including Minister of Culture Ismail and Minister of Defense Baydh. The resolutions from the Fourth Congress were not implemented since most radicals had been removed from the government.

Then trouble came from the exiled opposition who had found support from North Yemen and Saudi Arabia. Shabi needed help and had no choice but to let the radicals regroup and support him against the opposition forces. The radicals took advantage of the situation and forced Shabi to give up the presidency. He gave it to his cousin Faisal al-Shabi, who was soon ousted, too.

In June 1969, the radical wing of the NF gained power in what was called the "Corrective Movement." The leaders now sought to implement the resolutions outlined at the Fourth Congress. The first step was the establishment of collective leadership in the form of a five-man presidium: Salim Rubay Ali (president and chairman of the council), Haytham (prime minister), Ismail (NF secretary general), Ali Nasir Muhammad (defense minister), and Muhammad Salih Awlaqi. South Yemen was now a Marxist state, and in December 1970, it was renamed the People's Democratic Republic of Yemen.

In southern Yemen the city of Shibam is famous for its tall buildings built with mud bricks. Some of these buildings stand nine stories high.

6

Years of Conflict

After more than a century of British rule, South Yemen was free. It was an independent country and the people were able to choose their destiny. In North Yemen, the monarchy had been toppled and a new republic born.

In the north and south, the hope for independence had materialized and the dream of unity seemed within reach. Both states claimed to support the idea of a unified Yemen. However, the expectation of a merged state in the late 1960s did not unfold. The two states chose to take their independence and move in divergent directions. The south moved toward a socialist society and ties with the Soviet Union while the north remained a market economy and retained ties with Saudi Arabia. Given these two distinct Yemeni states, the North remained an internal problem to the South and the South stayed a problem for the North.

SALIM AND SOUTH YEMEN

Salim Rubay Ali stepped into the position of president and chairman of the council for the new government of South Yemen. A new constitution and a new name for the nation, People's Democratic Republic of Yemen (PDRY), were effected soon after. Then the real work began. Physical, as well as financial, rebuilding needed to be done. South Yemen was one of the poorest countries in the world. Despite covering an area equal in size to Britain, it had a small population of about two million and only a few of those were skilled workers. It had only a few miles of paved roads outside of Aden. Life expectancy was around 46 years and more than 50 percent of the population was illiterate.

In this time of need, Salim turned to the Western states and the Arab states, but could not obtain any significant amounts of aid. He asked China but they were unable to help. Next, Salim turned to the Soviet Union. There was no Arab state in the socialist bloc and therefore the Soviets were eager to provide economic and technical assistance to South Yemen.

Salim visited Moscow in November 1972 and signed military, economic, and cultural aid agreements. Within a few years, South Yemen became a steadfast Marxist state and began nationalizing the economy and society. In 1977, the USSR showed its strong support by shifting its regional naval base from Somalia to Aden. Salim also developed ties with Cuba and East Germany.

Under Salim, South Yemen was changing dramatically. Tribalism was oppressed. Tribal surnames were banned. Qat chewing was restricted. Polygamy was outlawed and women were allowed to remove their veils, and even encouraged to join the armed forces. However, the government in the south held very tight control of the people. They lived under police surveillance all day.

Tens of thousands of people left Aden. Perhaps as much as a quarter of the population left the PDRY.

Among the population who remained, Salim was very popular. In late November 1973 when he visited Shibam in Hadramaut, crowds lined up to dance and sing as his car passed by. But not everyone in the government liked Salim. In Aden, there were several opposing factions. One was made up of Northerners such as Abd al-Fattah Ismail. Another was Ali Nasir Muhammad of Dathinah, prime minister since 1971.

THE WAR OF 1972

Relations between North Yemen and South Yemen remained strained. Incidents between the armies of the two nations began to occur more frequently. Along the unmarked border, one group struck at another and then retaliation ensued. By the summer of 1972, the border skirmishes had engaged large units of armed forces on both sides. The war, however, did not last long. Mediation by the Arab League led to an agreement between the YAR and the PDRY in October. Besides ending the border war, the agreement contained a huge surprise. The two governments agreed to negotiate terms toward unification.

The goal was confirmed a month later when Salim and Iryani signed another agreement. The next step was for the two leaders to establish a series of joint committees to plan the details of the merger. The new country of Yemen would have a single capital and a single government, which implied equal legitimacy of the two existing governments.

In the North, the agreement only appealed to the political left. The tribal leadership knew that the NLF had stripped the power of old traditional leaders in the south and therefore they opposed the union. Saudi Arabia, fearing the political influence of a unified Yemen, also encouraged opposition. Given the various bodies of resistance, it became impossible to move forward with plans of unity.

THE YAR (NORTH YEMEN)

North Yemenis were beginning to feel in control of their own destiny. The first public elections in Yemen history were held in March 1971. The people elected the 179-member legislature called the Consultative Council. The new Yemen constitution, placed into effect on December 28, 1970, also made people feel hopeful. It embodied the thinking of the older generation of Free Yemenis. It declared Yemen to be an Islamic, as well as Arab, nation. It stated that the foundation of Yemeni society was the family, itself founded on religion, custom, and patriotism.

The compromise government of North Yemen attempted to implement a program of political and economic development. But with few resources and few skilled laborers it was difficult to implement changes. Then economic good fortune came along, unconnected to anything the YAR government had done. The discovery of oil in several Arabian states brought prosperity to the entire region. A huge flow of foreign aid came in and remittances from Yemenis working abroad greatly increased.

President Iryani focused on the economic needs of his

A traditional hut in the village of Tihamah in northern Yemen reflects the fact that Yemen remains largely an agricultural country.

people. He built financial institutions rather than work on the military or the state bureaucracy. He took few steps toward creating a civil service or toward equipping the armed forces or reforming the governmental bureaucracy. Of course, these were matters of great political sensitivity. For example, there were 13,000 bureaucrats in North Yemen in 1969 and 30,000 by the mid-1970s. To impose changes on this group might have been political suicide.

Iryani was a great politician, a scholar, and a poet, but he was unable to deal with the multitude of problems, both domestic and foreign. Eventually, the tribal alliances of the north lost patience with his government and enacted a bloodless coup on June 13, 1974.

The civilian cabinet was dismissed and replaced with a military-led cabinet. Ibrahim al-Hamdi was appointed the new president. He had such great charisma and political skills that within a few months he managed to win the support of or neutralize every major faction in the country. Thus, he paved the way for his reforms, which included economic development, elimination of corruption, centralization of political control, and an end to economic irresponsibility of the ministries and their projects.

The government's situation continued to be helped by the money flowing in from remittances of Yemenis working abroad and from increases in foreign aid. By the late 1970s, work was underway on a range of agricultural, infrastructure, and human resource development projects.

Another part of Hamdi's plan was Yemen unity. In early 1977 Hamdi and Salim met near the border for joint talks. In August, Salim came to Sana. They were planning to talk again in Aden in October, but Hamdi was murdered two days before the meeting.

Not all sectors of the North Yemen population had accepted the government's new powers and influence over traditional political, economic, and social relationships. By 1977, Saudi Arabia and nearly all the northern tribes thought that Hamdi was becoming too supportive of South Yemen and the reformist elements in the south of North Yemen. An unknown assassin killed Hamdi on October 11, 1977.

A few hours later, the Military Command Council

met and announced that the chief of staff, Colonel Ahmad al-Ghashmi, would be the new president. He took office and declared that there would be no changes to Hamid's policies and goals. But relations with South Yemen were terminated. Another change Ghashmi made was to eliminate the Military Command Council. This angered one member of the council, al-Alim, who felt he was being pushed out of the government. Al-Alim rebelled and Ali Abdullah Saleh, as military governor of Taiz, was sent to deal with the uprising. Saleh forced al-Alim to flee to South Yemen. But Ghashmi's problems were not over.

Under strange circumstances, Ghashmi was killed by a suitcase bomb on June 24, 1978. It was widely believed to have been the work of the socialist party in Aden.

THE SALEH ERA OF THE YAR

Because the Military Command Council had been eliminated, there was no immediate appointment of a new president in North Yemen. A presidential council was formed to select the next leader. It was not an easy task. Iryani had been forced out in 1974, Hamdi murdered just the past October, and now Ghashmi had been killed. They had to find someone willing to step into the line of fire. Saleh was elected.

There was great public skepticism about Saleh. Some thought he was doomed and doubted he would last six months. Others doubted his ability to stabilize the country and predicted that the YAR would dissolve.

Saleh had little formal education and was from a tribal background. But he had proven himself as an able soldier when his country had needed him. Saleh had been involved in the coup of 1962 that ousted the monarchy. Afterward he commanded a post on the road from

Mukha and was later promoted to commander at Taiz. He had helped bring Hamdi to power and put down the revolt of al-Alim against Hamdi. Now, Saleh was stepping into the position of president.

Relations between the Saleh regime and the PDRY began badly and led straight to a second border war in early 1979. The PDRY perceived that the cause of Marxism was in need of direct action in the Arab world. Thus, they helped to instigate and fund an opposition movement in the north, the National Democratic Front (NDF). This group allegedly instigated the assassination of Ghashmi in 1978. Ultimate responsibility for the killing fell on PDRY President Salim Rubay Ali and he was executed. Abd al-Fattah Ismail became President.

The basic conflicts between North Yemen and South Yemen appeared irreconcilable. The continuing tensions led to fighting and a brief war, in 1979. This was followed again by efforts on the part of other Arab states to bring about reconciliation. Particularly, the Arabs wanted to avoid intervention by the U.S. and the USSR. The efforts were successful in ending the fighting and once again produced talks of unification. The goal of unity was reaffirmed by the northern and southern heads of state during a summit meeting in Kuwait in March 1979. However, the PDRY continued promoting dissidence against the YAR.

Saleh proved to be a fierce foe. He was not able to gain complete control of the Saudi Arabia border or to end the kidnappings and hijackings by tribesmen, but his ability to exercise power within YAR borders and tribal lands was developing. Most importantly, his power was strong enough to defeat the PDRY-supported National Democratic Front. The NDF movement had spread over a wide area of the YAR by early 1980. The NDF was planting mines and engaging in terrorism. An armed rebellion finally erupted in 1982, but Saleh's government forces defeated it.

In November 1981, Saleh completed the draft of the constitution for a unified state that had been proposed in 1979. He took it to Aden and announced: "If unity is the answer to violence and terrorism, then so be it." Unity was again rejected but several other agreements between the two states were reached. During his visit, Saleh also made an important contact; he traveled to the Hadramaut and met Ali Salim al-Baydh, the leading socialist party member. The two men agreed to smooth the progress of the border crossing between North and South Yemen. The meeting appeared to signal the start of a new era of cooperative relations.

In North Yemen, Saleh established the People's General Congress (PGC). The party brought together a number of underground parties in an effort to present a united front to counterbalance the Yemen Socialist Party (YSP) in the South. But the single political party in the south was not as strong and united as it appeared.

CIVIL WAR IN SOUTH YEMEN

President Ismail was the major driving force behind the PDRY's move toward the Soviet Union. He was the leading ideologist of revolution and promoted scientific socialism. Ultimately, he became too tyrannical and rigid. In April 1980, Ismail resigned and went to Moscow. His successor was Ali Nasir Muhammad.

Stability was strengthened when Ali Nasir Muhammad assumed the Presidency and the positions of prime minister and secretary general of the YSP. Nasir Muhammad pursued a strategy of close cooperation with the Soviet Union and improved relations with his Arab neighbors. He stopped the government's support of the fighting against the regimes in the YAR and Oman.

He tried to improve the economy but severe floods in 1982, followed by droughts in 1983 and 1984, hurt agricultural efforts. The downturn in oil demand also resulted in loss of revenues from workers' remittances. The major source of the country's income continued to come from the Aden oil refinery and port bunkering and ship repair facilities.

Politically, South Yemen had established a one-party state, with the only party being the Yemen Socialist Party. Thus, if there was a struggle within the party, there was nowhere for adversaries to go. Unfortunately, there was a struggle within the YSP. Differences over party policy surged and people jostled for control. Nasir Muhammad's style did not help. He and his friends displayed fancy cars, new buildings, and piles of money while many people around the capital of Aden lived in shanties. One friend is said to have built a palace with gardens, swimming pool, and satellite television.

The split between the display of wealth and excesses by a few and the drought and poverty in the rural areas was widening. The two factions of the Yemen Socialist Party began buying weapons and equipment. They plotted against each other.

In a bold move, President Ali Nasir Muhammad tried to eliminate members of the opposing faction on January 13, 1986. According to an official account by the Aden Ministry of Culture, it was 10:20 A.M. when a special meeting of the Politburo was about to convene. Suddenly, Muhammad's personal guards walked in and fired a shot into Ali Antar, vice president and an opponent of the president.

The guards started firing at the other men in the room. Salih Muslih Qasim, Defense Minister, and Ali Shaiyia Hadi, Head of the Control Commission were

Collecting precious rainwater in anticipation of drought has been done for centuries. These reservoirs cut into hillsides to collect rain as it runs downhill were photographed in Aden in 1926.

killed. Ali Salim al-Baydh escaped by sliding down a rope of curtains. About the same time, a gunboat fired at the home of Ismail. He was not at home at the time, but he was later executed.

President Nasir Muhammad did not portray the events as outright murders; he made a public claim that the killings had been necessary to defeat an attempted coup.

He felt confident he would be successful in the purging of his opponents, especially if the YAR stayed out of it. To encourage such a position, he quickly sent a message to Saleh thanking him for not getting involved.

Six days later, Nasir Muhammad had a different message for Saleh. He was now formally asking Saleh to intervene, and in return, offering to announce unity of the two Yemens. Saleh refused the offer. He probably knew why the offer was forthcoming.

Nasir Muhammad had not realized that the ranks of the army were loyal to the opposition. Within a few days of the confrontation, they swung over to the other side. After ten days of fighting, Nasir Muhammad had no choice but to flee the country. Some 60,000 of his supporters followed him to the YAR.

It had been a bitter, hard-fought fight. There were thousands of casualties and tremendous economic and physical damage.

THE DISCOVERY OF OIL

While other Arab countries had opened their doors to oil exploration centuries earlier, Yemen had remained closed. Back in the 1920s, geologists suspected that there might be oil deposits in Yemen, but the few drillings that had been made near the Red Sea were unproductive. An American company had offered Imam Yahya two million dollars for exploration rights, but he refused, mainly because he feared he would later have trouble getting the foreigners out of Yemen. In the 1950s, Imam Ahmad allowed some oil exploration but nothing was found.

The Middle Eastern countries that had encouraged exploration were exporting huge amounts of oil by 1973. The increased revenues from oil and the development occurring in those countries attracted many workers from North Yemen and South Yemen. Saudi Arabia, in particular, required a large amount of imported labor. In 1982, the remittances from about 100,000 workers accounted for half of the Gross National Product (GNP) for South Yemen. In the early 1980s, an estimated one million North Yemenis working abroad sent home over a quarter of the GNP.

The situation changed dramatically as a result of the worldwide decline in demand for oil in the 1980s. In 1986 the two Yemen nations had the lowest per capita income in the Middle East and seemed likely to remain that way. They produced few products for export. Most of their income was derived from foreign remittances, loans, and grants from their rich Arab neighbors, the Soviet Union, Western nations, and international lending organizations. The strongest possibility for economic improvement existed in the hope of the discovery of oil in marketable quantities.

It seemed a strange turn of fate that this land that held the ancient riches of frankincense and myrrh should be the only Arab state not to hold buried reserves of oil. And, in fact, it turned out to be false. The territory along the ancient trade route—Marib, Shabwah, and Hadramaut—came into fame once again when oil was finally discovered in Yemen.

In 1984, the Yemen Hunt Oil Company, a group of firms from North Yemen, the U.S., and South Korea, announced that it had located oil fields about 70 kilometers northeast of Marib. The company started digging the first rig in the Marib-al Jawf Zone on January 30, 1984. On July 8, it was announced that the daily average production was 7,800 barrels. North Yemen officials estimated that the production would rise to between 100,000 and 200,000 barrels a day.

Though the magnitude of the discovery was small by world standards, it was significant to Yemen. It could provide a source of energy and create government revenues. The prospect for the North Yemen economy looked promising as additional drilling started to determine the extent of the oil fields. It was thought that the fields might even extend into South Yemen.

In early 1985, the Yemen Hunt Oil Company announced that it would build a small refinery to supply the domestic oil market and a crude oil pipeline to ship exports to the coast. Work started on the construction of the Marib refinery in September 1985, and by April 1986 President Saleh inaugurated the Marib facility. The refinery was expected to satisfy up to half of the country's need for fuel oil, gasoline, and diesel, saving the YAR about $120 million annually in petroleum imports.

The pipeline extended 250 miles from the Marib region to the Red Sea. Oil began to flow through the new pipeline on December 9, 1987. Production reached the predicted 200,000 barrels per day in 1988. It was hoped that the production could be increased to 400,000 barrels per day. The estimated $600 million per year in revenue helped make up for the loss in remittances caused by the sharp decline in production in other oil-rich nations.

The discovery of oil brought economic improvement to North Yemen. In turn, this brought funds for development and modernization. The OPEC Fund for International Development provided $4 million to finance a highway project and the Abu Dhabi Fund for Arab Economic Development gave $10 million to help finance a port expansion project at Hodeida. The World Bank's International Development Association loaned $10 million for a project to increase agricultural productivity. The United States and the Soviet Union provided aid over the years, as did Saudi Arabia and Kuwait.

WORK TOWARD UNIFICATION

While North Yemen was enjoying prosperity, South Yemen's economic situation had grown worse, partly as a result of the civil war. The task of rebuilding fell to President Haider Abubaker al-Attas, a 49-year-old engineer, and Baydh, secretary of the Yemen Socialist Party. They would have to rely on their Soviet friends for an enormous amount of aid.

The good news for the PDRY was that Yemen was of strategic importance to the Soviets. Since 1979, when it signed a 20-year friendship treaty with Moscow, the PDRY was home to the only Soviet military presence in the Middle East. The Soviet naval base and submarine pens in Aden and the communications facility manned by East Germans were significant operations. And when the extension of the Aden airport runway was completed, the Russians would have the capability to launch long-range surveillance aircraft from Yemen. It seemed certain that the Soviets would bail out South Yemen in order to defend their military privileges there.

The new regime of al-Attas tried to ally itself with the idea of Yemeni unification but the YAR refused to convene talks. The civil war in the south had put a strain on the north since ex-President Muhammad and thousands of his followers had taken refuge in the YAR. Al-Attas and his leaders in Aden were unwilling to reconcile with the ex-president and ease the refugee burden. Thus, talks about unity went nowhere.

A serious crisis unfolded in late 1987 when tensions broke out in the disputed borderland. Reports indicated that oil exploration teams were conducting surveys in the area for the PDRY and the YAR. Both sides massed their armed forces in the area in March 1988. In mid-April, a summit meeting was held between President Saleh and YSP Secretary General Baydh. On May 4, after another summit, the two leaders signed major agreements.

Once again a border dispute had brought the two sides to mediation. Perhaps this time it was no big surprise when they came away talking about unification. One of the agreements called for reviving the draft of the unity constitution and forming a joint committee for a unified political organization. Another agreement provided for the free movement of Yemenis between the two Yemens.

As in past instances, the two Yemens pledged allegiance to unity but seemed to take very small steps toward making it happen. Nevertheless, the immediate crisis of the border dispute was diffused before it escalated into serious fighting. Just days after the May 4 agreements, a committee of senior officers from the two Yemens supervised the withdrawal of forces from the borderland, and the tensions of the previous months quickly subsided. Everyone expected the rhetoric of unity to subside, too, as it had throughout Yemen's history.

This time it did not. Conditions were different. The Soviet empire was dissolving and their aid to South Yemen stopped. The PDRY found itself bankrupt and turned to North Yemen for help. This was also a prudent move because of the oil discoveries in the desert along the border of the two countries. By 1989, the two countries were moving toward unification.

In November 1989, Saleh of the YAR and Baydh of the PDRY agreed on a draft of the unity constitution originally drawn up in 1981. The Republic of Yemen was declared on May 22, 1990. Ali Abdullah Saleh became President and Ali Salim al-Baydh became Vice President. It seemed a miracle that unity finally came to Yemen and that these two men were alive to make it happen. When Saleh took office in 1978, he was expected to last six months. Somehow he had survived 12 years and dozens of assassination attempts. As for Baydh, if he had not escaped that January day in 1986, he would have been dead.

President Ali Abdullah Saleh casts his ballot on Tuesday, February 20, 2001 during local elections that included proposals to amend the constitution.

7
The Republic of Yemen

The Republic of Yemen was a new country in the process of modernizing and opening up to the outside world. Elementary education became widely available. People, even women, were allowed to vote. Women also drove cars and watched television. Friends communicated on cell phones. Yet the country also maintained much of its tribal character and old ways. Sheiks still settled disputes ranging from family spats to murder. People still tended flocks of goats and sheep, and most marriages were still arranged by the families of the couple. Male highlander's carried a handcrafted dagger, called a djambia, and a gun as part of the dress code. Many women wore black robes that covered them from head to toe, with only a narrow slit for their eyes.

Saleh tried to bring stability and economic growth to this new country. He tried to move Yemen toward a new era of peace and prosperity. But if peace did not last, the survival of the Republic of Yemen would be doomed.

A 30-month transitional period for completing the unification of the two political and economic systems was set. Together, the 26-member YAR advisory council and the 17-member PDRY presidium elected a presidential council. The presidential council then appointed a Prime Minister, who formed a cabinet. There was also a 301-seat provisional unified Parliament, consisting of 159 members from the north, 111 members from the south, and 31 other members appointed by the chairman of the council. In a decision that resulted in dire consequences, the northern and southern armed forces were not integrated; they remained under separate commands.

The union was tenuous during the transition period. President Saleh and Vice President Baydh had dissimilar ideas about how the country should be managed and how political power should be shared. In addition, the mixture of ex-Marxist politicians with tribal leaders caused considerable stress in the fragile political arena. Forty political parties vied for popular support. Financial problems had been inherited from the South, which had made $6.5 billion in arms purchases from the Soviet Union. Then, Saudi Arabia expelled more than a million workers because of Yemen's support of Iraq in its invasion of Kuwait. Not even the weather cooperated; there were periods of floods and droughts.

The general populace proved their support by ratifying the unity constitution on May 15, 1991. About 98 percent of the voters cast votes in favor of the constitution, the first article of which stated "the Republic of Yemen is a sovereign and independent state. It is indivisible and inalienable. The Yemeni people are an integral part of the Arab nation and the Islamic world." It affirmed Yemen's commitment to free elections, a multiparty political system, the right to own private property, equality under the law, and respect of basic human rights.

The first parliamentary elections were held on April 27, 1993. International groups assisted in the organization of the elections and observed actual balloting. They declared the elections were "free and fair." The General People's Congress (GPC) received the most votes and the Islah party, composed of various Yemeni tribal and religious groups, came in second. The Yemen Socialist Party came in third but the leader, Baydh, tried to keep his party's posts and privileges. He began to stir up discontent against unity and against Saleh.

In addition to political differences, personal animosity existed between Saleh and Baydh. Both men were extremely astute and ambitious, and a clash of egos was almost inevitable. Baydh saw Saleh as unresponsive to the south. There had been about 150 assassinations of YSP leaders and Saleh was unwilling to arrest and prosecute the alleged killers. Baydh also accused Saleh of taking profits from oil operations in the south, which he did not want to share with the north. On the other hand, Saleh believed Baydh and the YSP held unrealistic aspirations for the south. With only a fifth of the population, the south seemed determined to maintain a 50 percent stake in power.

In August 1993 Baydh protested by staying in Aden and refusing to go to Sana to take the oath of office as vice president. Baydh's absence paralyzed the government and heightened tensions throughout Yemen. Security broke down and political rivals and tribal elements fought.

Then, suddenly on February 20, 1994 negotiations between northern and southern leaders resulted in the signing of the document of accord in Amman, Jordan. Unity was back on track and the Yemeni people were relieved. Some cried tears of joy. Others thanked God.

THE CIVIL WAR OF 1994

Peace did not last. The very next day the two armies exchanged gunfire. On May 4, full-scale civil war erupted. Bombs and artillery shells exploded into the sky above Aden. Gunfire rang through the streets. Northern war-planes attacked the airport in Aden while southern planes struck at the Sana airport and the presidential palace. Power outages darkened houses and emergency generators were put into use at hotels and hospitals. Water and telephone services were cut off to most of the country. Schools and businesses were closed.

"Unity is dead," said one official.

President Saleh ordered a 30-day state of emergency and a ban on carrying firearms or shooting in the streets. It had no effect. The fierce fighting continued. It was estimated that 12,000 people had been killed in just four days of fighting. Thousands of foreigners fled Yemen.

The northern army held a numerical edge, about 40,000 northern troops against 20,000 southern troops. Some observers expected Aden to fall quickly. But southern resistance was resolute, and southern commanders had greater air power. It was reported that the southern air force had 2,500 men and 120 combat aircraft, while the northern force had only 1,000 men and just 73 planes. The south's artillery included Scud missiles, which they fired toward Sana. One missed the presidential palace and slammed into a block of houses, killing 25 civilians.

On May 21, southern leaders declared secession and the establishment of the Democratic Republic of Yemen (DRY). Baydh proclaimed himself president of the new republic. Skeptical supporters started deserting after this announcement. The international community refused to recognize the DRY.

Aden was captured on July 7, 1994. The resistance movement collapsed and thousands of southern leaders and military personnel went into exile. President Saleh tried to reconcile the country by announcing a general amnesty, and most southerners eventually returned to Yemen. Baydh fled to Oman with several million dollars in cash.

THE STRUGGLE FOR PEACE AND PROSPERITY

Saleh had won the war and the Yemeni people were united again. But it had come at a great cost of human lives and an estimated $11 billion in damage.

President Ali Abdullah Saleh was elected by Parliament on October 1, 1994 to a five-year term. In the Parliamentary elections of April 1997, the GPC won a majority of the seats. Saleh, who continued to serve as President, was seen as the great unifying figure of Yemen. In the first direct elections for the presidency, held on September 23, 1999, it was not surprising that Saleh won more than 96 percent of the ballots cast. His opponents reportedly boycotted the election.

The political environment was improving but economic conditions were not as promising. The high expectations for new oil discoveries in the late 1980s had been dampened. Many major oil companies had signed exploration agreements that were extremely advantageous for the Yemen government. They included large bonuses and work programs in the expectation of large oil discoveries being made in the area. However, the results were disappointing.

A few small discoveries were made but the general outlook was not hopeful. Some of the major companies left Yemen. Others scaled down their operations. By 2000, the Hunt Oil Company field near Marib had run out. One bright spot was the CanadianOxy operation in the east near al-Mukalla, which was pumping 210,000 barrels a day and expecting to increase its output.

As Yemen became more open to the outside world, foreign oil workers, government officials, and even tourists visited the country. In December 1998, a convoy of Western tourists was driving near the southern town of Mawdiyah, about 175 miles south of Sana. Suddenly, some men fired at the police escort and said they would shoot the tourists if the police did not back away. The men then took the 16 tourists and led them toward a mountain hideout.

While this may seem like an atrocious incident, kidnappings are not uncommon in Yemen and hardly ever lead to any harm of the hostages. Foreigners are taken to win concessions from the government. In exchange for the release of a hostage, tribesmen might ask for new roads, some water, a school, or more telephone lines. The hostages are generally treated as kindly as guests and are released unharmed.

This kidnapping was the first reported incident in Yemen involving the abduction of foreigners by a fanatical Islamic group. Security officials said the men belonged to the Islamic Jihad, an extremist terrorist gang. The kidnappers had purely political motives; they demanded the release of their leader, Saleh Haidara al-Atwi.

As the kidnappers led their hostages up the mountain, a group of Yemeni soldiers were in pursuit. The army approached and the kidnappers, armed with rifles and grenade launchers, grew tense. Then there was gunfire from somewhere. Exactly what happened is unclear. One report said the soldiers fired first. Then the kidnappers made the hostages stand in front of them and raise their hands up. The hostages had no choice but to serve as human shields. Some of the shots hit the tourists. As the abductors fled, they turned and killed two captives.

Yemeni officials insisted that the kidnappers began

The beauty of cities such as Sana draws foreign tourists and has occasionally put them in danger of being taken hostage for ransom or gains of some sort. Most of these incidents end peacefully, but in 1998 a fanatical Islamic group abducted sixteen tourists and when it was over four hostages had died and two more were injured.

shooting the hostages. Only then did the troops open fire. Whichever story is true, the result remains the same. Four hostages were dead: three British citizens and one Australian. One American woman was shot in the hip and one British woman was shot in the shoulder. The other ten hostages escaped unharmed.

THE USS *COLE* BOMBING

In 1998, Yemen and the United States held their first joint military exercises. The U.S. also provided help with clearing mines left from the 1994 civil war. There have been

American involvement in Yemen is unpopular with extremist Islamic groups. The suicide bombing of the USS *Cole* by two men in a small boat loaded with explosives killed seventeen soldiers and injured thirty-nine others. The bombing appeared to be the work of an armed Islamic group.

occasional visits to Yemen by U.S. ships and by senior officers. In 1999, the U.S. Defense Department transferred its Red Sea strategic fuel storage depot from Djibouti to Aden. One reason for this move was that the Djibouti harbor was crowded and refueling could take ten times as long as at Aden. Another reason was political; the U.S. wanted to cultivate a relationship with Yemen.

This American involvement in Yemen was unpopular with the extremist Islamic groups. In November 1999, members of such a group planned to attack a group of U.S. military personnel. The plan was thwarted. Another attack, planned against the Royal Hotel in Aden where American servicemen were staying, was also unsuccessful. In January 2000, a bombing of the USS *Sullivans* failed when the weight of the explosives almost sank the small boat attempting the sabotage. On October 12, 2000, the attack against the USS *Cole* succeeded.

The USS *Cole*, a guided-missile destroyer, was moored 600 meters offshore from Aden at a waterborne platform designed specifically for refueling operations. After the ship began the refueling process, a small boat carrying two men approached. Then there was a huge explosion.

The small boat was believed to have been filled with 400-700 pounds of explosives. The bombers used C-4, a military explosive that is most effective at blasting through metal. The blast blew a 40-by-40-foot hole in the side of the USS *Cole*, causing $240 million in damage. The bombing killed seventeen sailors and injured thirty-nine people.

One U.S. official called what the two suicide bombers had done "a senseless act of terrorism." U.S. Ambassador Barbara Bodine said it was a tragedy and "an insult." From the terrorists point of view it was likely seen as a shrewd and determined act of violence that demonstrated the vulnerabilities of even a superpower like the U.S.

Based on the belief that the perpetrators were from abroad, the Yemen government categorized the act as "imported terrorism." It worked with the U.S. officials on the investigation of the incident and the hunt for the instigators. No credible group claimed responsibility for the assault. It appeared to be the work of an armed Islamic group rather than a non-religious political organization. Its purpose seemed to be part of a general protest against American involvement in the Middle East. Armed Islamic groups frequently have (or claim to have) some link to Osama bin Laden and the al-Qaeda network.

U.S. investigators focused suspicion on Osama bin Laden. Bin Laden denied any involvement in the attack but was said to be pleased about it. A newspaper reported that he "knelt and thanked God for this operation, which has shaken the American military reputation."

OSAMA BIN LADEN AND TERRORISM

The suicide bombing of the USS *Cole* in the port of Aden was another incident in a string of terrorist attacks: the 1993 World Trade Center bombing, the 1996 killing of nineteen soldiers in Saudi Arabia, and the 1998 bombings in Kenya and Tanzania. Then, on September 11, 2001, terrorists attacked the World Trade Center in New York City and the Pentagon in Washington, D.C. The chief suspect in all of these attacks was Osama bin Laden.

News reporters flooded into the little town of Ribat Baashen in the Hadramaut province of Yemen. This is the ancestral village of the bin Laden family. But the townspeople tell the journalists that no one there knows Osama bin Laden and he never set foot in their village. The last bin Laden to live there was Abdullah, an uncle to Osama, but he left in 1969 when South Yemen became a Marxist state.

Osama bin Laden's father left Yemen in 1925. He went to Saudi Arabia and operated a prosperous construction business. The bin Laden family is considered the wealthiest non-royal family in Saudi Arabia.

Osama was born in Saudi Arabia and grew up there. He left in 1969 to fight against the Soviets in Afghanistan. After the Soviets withdrew in 1989, he returned to Saudi Arabia to work in the family construction business. He was expelled in 1991 for his anti-government activities, in particular, he had strongly objected to the presence of U.S. troops in Saudi Arabia during the Gulf War. He spent the next five years in Sudan until that government expelled him. He returned to Afghanistan where he received protection from the ruling powers, the Taliban militia. By then he had already formed a terrorist network known as al-Qaeda, meaning "the Base." This group consisted mainly of militant Islams. It reportedly had thousands of followers all over the world, from Saudi Arabia to Bosnia to the Philippines to Yemen.

The U.S. State Department calls Osama bin Laden "one of the most significant sponsors of Islamic extremist activities in the world today." And they consider Somalia and Yemen to be potential havens for extremists. One U.S. counter-terrorist official described Yemen as having the second largest al-Qaeda network outside of Afghanistan.

Yemen seems to make an attractive haven. The mountainous terrain is a good base for military training operations and for hideouts. Weapons are readily available. Security in many parts of the country is minimal. Its land and sea borders are virtually impossible to guard, making it easy to slip in and out of the country undetected. Many Muslim fighters took refuge in Yemen after the Afghan war.

One group operating in Yemen called itself the Islamic Army of Aden. In 1998, they openly declared war on U.S. interests in Yemen and announced their support of Osama bin Laden. This group probably contained Islamic Jihad elements from the previous Islamic Army of Aden-Abyan. Yemeni police and military troops had attacked their camp, but the effectiveness of the effort was unknown.

In retrospect, some officials suspect that the Jihad may have been responsible for some of the 150 murders of Yemen Socialist Party leaders in 1992-94. These killings were a crucial factor leading to the civil war in 1994.

THE FUTURE OF YEMEN

On May 22, 2000, the Republic of Yemen celebrated ten years of unification. To some observers, the capital of Sana might have looked like it was hosting a security exercise rather than a party. Officials shut off the mobile phone network so agitators could not communicate. Some roads near Sana were closed. About 25,000 troops patrolled the streets, with some carrying AK-47s. Hospitals were put on high alert.

The celebration went smoothly and foreign dignitaries were kept safe during their stays in Yemen. However, the extravaganza upset some critics of the government. The party cost millions of dollars, and in a country with so much poverty, it seemed an abuse of wealth and power.

However, the celebration did serve as a way to improve relations with one guest: Crown Prince Abdullah of Saudi Arabia. The Saudi's hostile attitude toward Yemen unity seemed to be thawing. Three weeks after the prince's visit, both countries signed an agreement that defined the entire Saudi-Yemeni border.

Shortly thereafter, at the Millenium Summit at the United Nations, President Saleh expressed his aspirations. He said: "Now at the threshold of the twenty-first century, Yemen is at peace with itself and its neighbors. Peace in the country and in the region is the objective of Yemen policy, which concentrates on solving the border problems with its neighbors through dialogue, understanding, or arbitration. . . . We are looking forward to a new age of cooperation in our region and the world."

Within the country, Saleh took steps toward further democratization. The government had already conducted direct elections for the lower house of parliament and for the president. The first local government elections were held in February 2001. Unfortunately they did not go as smoothly as the previous elections. There were 26,000 candidates competing for 7,000 seats. Just the task of organizing the election was enormous. Quarrels between candidates and complaints of misconduct were rampant. Voting was prevented from taking place in 200 polling stations, either by violence or problems with the ballot boxes. At least 45 people, including several candidates, died on election day.

To try to restore people's faith in the government, Saleh shuffled his cabinet. Seventeen ministers lost their jobs

President Saleh (center) with new members of his government after a major reshuffling of his cabinet in 2001. Among the newcomers was Yemen's first woman minister, Professor Waheeba Fare, Rector of Queen Arwa University, who became the head of human rights. She is standing to the immediate left of Saleh in this picture.

and twenty-two newcomers were given posts. Among the newcomers was Yemen's first woman minister, Professor Waheeba Fare, Rector of Queen Arwa University, who became the head of human rights. At the swearing-in ceremony, Saleh emphasized to the new ministers the need to subdue corruption and to fulfil the people's aspirations in education, development and industry.

Saleh and the ministers have several internal problems to deal with. Saleh has managed to hold the union together but the political arena remains somewhat unstable, as demonstrated in the 2001 elections. Oil fields and oil refineries brought wealth to Yemen but not of the magnitude anticipated. Yemen remains a largely agricultural country. A modern Marib Dam was built in 1986, with hopes to revive the great irrigation system of the ancient Yemen. More than half of the population works in farming, yet Yemen relies heavily on imported foods.

Part of the problem is qat. Many farmers have converted their coffee or wheat fields to growing qat. Not much land and water are left for growing food. For the farmers, it makes sense. Qat can be replanted four times a year and there is a ready market for it. About 80 percent of the population chews qat. This widespread qat chewing is another concern for Yemen. Health experts fear that money is spent on qat instead of food, and businesses fear that qat is reducing productivity.

Some people say qat has been good for the economy. It is a highly developed industry and brings good profits to many Yemeni farmers. These profits have been used to improve irrigation systems and roadways.

The Yemeni people are holding on to their unique identity, such as qat chewing, yet struggling to find their place in the changing world. Tribes are still the dominant feature of Yemeni life and tribal loyalty is placed above all else except religion. But the outside world has once again pulled back the veil of seclusion and brought Yemen into the limelight.

Yemen's fame in the ancient world came from frankincense and coffee, but today it comes from guns and terrorists. There are over 17 million people and 50 million guns. Automatic rifles, shoulder-fired antiaircraft missile launchers, and hand grenades are sold at weekly markets. Guns are part of the male dress code, even for teenage boys. But the atmosphere of the world has changed since September 11, 2001. Terrorism has become the number one concern of the international community.

Tribes in the Marib, al-Jawf, and Shabwah regions are said to be sheltering al-Qaeda members. At the moment, Yemen is eager to cooperate with the U.S. in its hunt for these terrorists. In exchange, Yemen will get money, weapons, and military training.

Though the U.S. considered it risky, Vice President

Dick Cheney flew to Yemen on March 14, 2002, and met with President Saleh. They discussed the American military advisors that will soon be arriving in Yemen. Though the Yemeni people understand the importance of having training, they do not want Americans fighting in Yemen, and simply their presence in the country may turn public opinion against the United States. Cheney and Saleh also discussed another difficult subject: Iraq. While the U.S. is mobilizing support for actions against Iraq, Saleh is opposed to any U.S. military operation against Iraq.

Perhaps Saleh hears the echoes of his words: "We are looking forward to a new age of cooperation in our region and the world." No doubt he wants to cooperate. Yemen remains dependent on foreign aid, wages from Yemenis working abroad, and oil refinery operations. But the Yemeni people remain fiercely independent and resistant to foreign intervention in their affairs. (The day after Cheney's visit, a man threw two grenades at the U.S. Embassy in Sana.) The Yemeni also know that as the most populated country on the Arabian Peninsula, and the only democracy, they hold an important status.

"Yemen is at peace with itself and its neighbors," said Saleh. At least for the moment that is true. And Saleh deserves credit for it. He made his dream of unity come true and brought momentous opportunity for Yemen. He has the country on the brink of economic prosperity and political stability. If unity can survive, if disputes can be settled with dialogue, and if Yemen and the world powers can find a way to cooperate, the days of *Arabia Felix* may return.

570   Marib Dam breaks, signaling the decline of the Kingdom of Saba.

628   Islam is introduced to Yemen.

1839   British seize Aden.

1849   Ottoman Turks occupy northern Yemen.

1869   The Suez Canal opens.

1873   The Ottoman forces in Yemen begin to encroach on areas of British influence.

1891   The Zaydi imam begins uprisings against Ottoman rule.

1905   Ottoman and British powers divide Yemen into north and south.

1918   North Yemen becomes independent and Imam Yahya becomes ruler.

1948   Rebels assassinate Imam Yahya and his son Ahmad becomes imam.

1954   British construct oil refinery in Aden.

1962   North Yemen republican forces defeat the imam's royalist forces. North Yemen becomes the independent Yemen Arab Republic.

1962   Aden joins the British-created Federation of South Arabia.

1967   National Liberation Front forces British to leave South Yemen.

1970   South Yemen becomes People's Democratic Republic of Yemen, a Marxist state.

1972   Border conflicts are followed by unity talks, but unification does not ensue.

1978   North Yemen President Hamdi and his successor, Ghashmi, are killed. Saleh becomes president.

1978   Ismail takes power in South Yemen.

1984   Oil is discovered in North Yemen.

1986   Civil war erupts in South Yemen.

1990 On May 22, the two Yemen nations unite and form the Republic of Yemen.

1994 Civil war breaks out in May. Saleh's troops defeat the secessionists.

1998 Extremist Islamic group kidnaps foreign tourists. Four hostages are killed.

2000 The USS *Cole* navy ship is bombed in the Aden harbor.

2002 Yemen government cooperates in the international hunt for terrorists.

BOOKS:

Dresch, Paul. *A History of Modern Yemen.* Cambridge, United Kingdom: Cambridge University Press, 2000.

Mackintosh-Smith, Tim. *Yemen: The Unknown Arabia.* Woodstock, NY: The Overlook Press, 2000.

Wenner, Manfred W. *The Yemen Arab Republic: Development and Change in an Ancient Land.* Boulder, CO: Westview Press, Inc., 1991.

ON THE WEB:

www.al-bab.com

www.britannica.com

www.news.bbc.co.uk

www.yemeninfo.gov.ye

Badeeb, Saeed M. *Saudi-Egyptian Conflict over North Yemen, 1962-1970.* Boulder, CO: Westview Press and Washington, D.C.: American-Arab Affairs Council, 1986.

Cockburn, Andrew. "Yemen United," *National Geographic.* April 2000, pp. 30-53.

Dresch, Paul. *A History of Modern Yemen.* Cambridge, United Kingdom: Cambridge University Press, 2000.

Hestler, Anna. *Cultures of the World: Yemen.* New York: Marshall Cavendish, 1999.

Little, Tom. *South Arabia: Arena of Conflict.* New York: Frederick A. Praeger, 1968.

Mackintosh-Smith, Tim. *Yemen: The Unknown Arabia.* Woodstock, NY: The Overlook Press, 2000.

Mulloy, Martin. *North Yemen.* New York: Chelsea House Publishers, 1987.

Nyrop, editor. *The Yemens: Country Studies.* Washington, D.C.: United States Government, Foreign Area Studies, The American University, 1986.

Schmidt, Dana Adams. *Yemen: The Unknown War.* New York: Holt, Rinehart and Winston, 1968.

Stookey, Robert W. *Yemen: The Politics of the Yemen Arab Republic.* Boulder, CO: Westview Press, 1978.

Wenner, Manfred W. *The Yemen Arab Republic: Development and Change in an Ancient Land.* Boulder, CO: Westview Press, Inc., 1991.

WEB SITE SOURCES:

www.al-bab.com

www.britannica.com

www.gpc.org.ye

www.historychannel.com

www.internationalspecialreports.com

www.news.bbc.co.uk

www.nic.gov.ye

www.nytimes.com

www.yemeninfo.gov.ye

www.yementimes.com

www.yemenia.com.ye

page:

2:   AP/Wide World Photos
17:   ©Magellan Geographix
18:   AP/Wide World Photos
23:   © AFP/Corbis
25:   © Inge Yspeert/Corbis
27:   AP/Wide World Photos
30:   © Michael Maslaa Historic
       Photographs/Corbis
34:   © Francoise de Mulder/Corbis
37:   © Bettmann/Corbis
39:   Hulton Archive by Getty Images
42:   © Francoise de Mulder/Corbis
46:   © Eye Ubiquitous/Corbis
49:   Hulton-Deutsch Collection/Corbis
53:   Hulton Archive by Getty Images

56:   © Francoise de Mulder/Corbis
60:   Hulton Deutsch Collection/Corbis
63:   © Bettmann/Corbis
68:   Hulton Deutsch Collection/Corbis
71:   © Bettmann/Corbis
76:   © Bettmann/Corbis
80:   © Earl Kowall/Corbis
85:   © Tiziana and Gianni Baldizzone/
       Corbis
91:   Hulton Deutsch Collection/Corbis
98:   AP/Wide World Photos
105:   AP/Wide World Photos
106:   AP/Wide World Photos
111:   © AFP Corbis

Cover: AP Photo/Kamran Jebreili

SANDRA WEBER is a writer and lecturer. She has an M.B.A from Temple University and a B.S. from Clarkson University. She is the author of three history books and numerous magazine articles.

AKBAR S. AHMED holds the Ibn Khaldun Chair of Islamic Studies at the School of International Service of American University. He is actively involved in the study of global Islam and its impact on contemporary society. He is the author of many books on contemporary Islam, including *Discovering Islam: Making Sense of Muslim History and Society,* which was the basis for a six-part television program produced by the BBC called *Living Islam.* Ahmed has been visiting professor and the Stewart Fellow in the Humanities at Princeton University, as well as visiting professor at Harvard University and Cambridge University.